GANG
redux

**A Balanced
Anti-Gang
Strategy**

JAMES DIEGO VIGIL
University of California, Irvine

WAVELAND

PRESS, INC.

Long Grove, Illinois

For information about this book, contact:
Waveland Press, Inc.
4180 IL Route 83, Suite 101
Long Grove, IL 60047-9580
(847) 634-0081
info@waveland.com
www.waveland.com

10-digit ISBN 1-57766-654-2
13-digit ISBN 978-1-57766-654-7

Printed in the United States of America

7 6 5 4 3 2 1

GANG
redux

Father Boyle enjoying community residents

Contents

Foreword

For nearly a quarter of a century, Diego Vigil and I have arm wrestled over this gang issue. Together in the classroom, in my office, on panels, walking in the "Projects," and over a beer in his home (with his luminous wife, Polly), we have sought to make sense of the root causes of gangs and how communities ought to address this sensibly. As the Founder and Executive Director of Homeboy Industries, the largest gang intervention program in the United States, and as a priest who has buried 168 human beings killed because of gang violence, it is clear to me that the search for answers and solutions is pressing indeed.

Gang violence is an enormously complex social dilemma, requiring from us all a reverence for its complexity. If we can stand in awe of what the poor have to carry, and not in judgment of how they carry it, chances are we will do right by this issue. In all of Vigil's work, he has sought to underscore the power of multiple marginality, the treacherous waters of street socialization and every imaginable contour of why and how young people find themselves caught in the gravitational "push" toward gang life. Diego Vigil has always had the healthiest respect for the complexity of gangs and no less so in this current, seminal text.

Since gangs are the places kids go when they have encountered their lives as a misery (and misery loves company), addressing the fonts of that misery requires attention to a great many factors. It also requires "all hands on deck" as we seek to do so. Acknowledging that no hopeful kid will join a gang, we can no longer place our trust in a "suppression only" approach. It has become abundantly clear that no kid is seeking anything when he/she joins a gang—each kid is always fleeing something. That truth colors what we choose to do.

Beyond calling for a merely comprehensive approach (as everyone does these days), Vigil urges communities to embrace a balanced response. He acknowledges that we need to right and correct our course in order to give due attention to the areas we have long neglected as we placed all our eggs in the "enforcement only" basket. With extraordinary clarity, Diego Vigil guides the reader to weigh all the necessary responses to the gang issue—as it relates to prevention and intervention and quickens communities to see the highest aerial view of this multi-faceted gang problem.

This is an important addition to Diego Vigil's already considerable contribution to the public discussion of gangs. He pushes us toward balance, and this could not be more timely. We all have learned from the mistakes made in previous decades. This work compels the reader to seek healthier communities by being smarter on crime, confident to take the long view, always reverent of complexity, and dedicated to what is balanced and sensible. After decades of contention, futility, and considerable "arm wrestling," *Gang Redux* allows us to find room for hope.

Father Gregory J. Boyle

Preface

Gang Redux, the title of the book, means returning to a former time when gangs were not as lethal as they are today and anti-gang strategies were more child-centered and balanced. Thus, I believe that to address the gang problem we must advocate for a balanced approach, utilizing prevention, intervention, and law enforcement as needed. This book begins by describing how poverty and marginalization lead to "street socialization" (i.e., being raised in the streets) and the generation of street gangs and gang members. Street socialization, in turn, undermines and transforms the normal course of human development where physical, cognitive, and social/emotional attributes result in unconventional lifestyles. In addition, street ways help institutionalize a street subculture. Before we can develop the prevention, intervention, and suppression strategies needed, we must look to these gang roots by examining the historical and cultural experiences of ethnic minority youths. Establishing the realities of time, place, and people will inform the formulation and implementation of remedial strategies.

We must focus on the social neglect, ostracism, economic marginalization, and cultural repression that residents in gang neighborhoods confront daily. The phrase "multiple marginality" reflects the complexities and persistence of these forces. Human developmental processes, as expected, are considerably altered and undermined under marginalization and street socialization circumstances. To reverse these situations and conditions the facts of time, place, and people can serve as a template for a balanced strategy.

Time: Stealing time away from the urban youths who are most susceptible to street socialization can begin by implementing programs and activities targeted at the three most important social control institutions of our society: homes and families, schools and teachers, and law enforcement and police. Time and timing is the issue not only with respect to the general time available to youth, i.e., where and with whom they spend it, how and what they do, but also for the key points in their life that are "time" pivotal to their growth and human development, changeable because youths can make choices that take them in either conventional or unconventional paths.

Place: Motivated offenders, suitable targets, and an absence of capable guardians converge in certain times and places to increase the possibility of a crime; such places are known as "hot spots." To address this, we would get rid of the present either/or situation of gang turf (where there is always the possibility of the occurrence of crime and violence) or stable, nongang turf (where neighborhoods are basically free from criminal activity) by setting up situations (i.e., social and personal outlets) and conditions (i.e., buildings and safe houses) that reestablish the character and identity of the (gang) neighborhood. During the 1960s' War on Poverty a similar idea was implemented in the form of the Teen Posts where the greater Los Angeles area had about 135 Teen posts.

People: It is self-evident by now that when time management is rearranged and the power of place reconfigured (or reformed and restructured!), people are the essence of the equation for change. The pool of people who can join the fight for community health is large.

Time, Place, and People for a Balanced Strategy: Law enforcement and suppression tactics, already overtaxed as a solution to a problem they did not cause, are having only limited success in addressing the gang problem. A focus on the roots of the problem will generate logical solutions that will aim not merely to stem the worst violence but also to begin the long hard march to regain social control and balance the present formula to include prevention and intervention. In tandem, and as needed, prevention, intervention, and law enforcement strategies can be utilized throughout the life of the individual, taking heed of human developmental issues. Concentrating on what youths do with their time, with whom they do it, along with the places where these activities occur and the people involved in them, is a very solid start.

Students in my courses at the University of California, Irvine, helped immensely by identifying prevention, intervention, and suppression programs and to them I extend a grateful thank you. Among them were those who provided special assistance: Heidi Bojorquez, Fatima Langmesser, Joseph Knox, Christian Peralta, Chris Rosales, Corey Attaway, Andrew Eng, Eddy M. Gana, Jr., Laura Buendia, Tatiana Diaz, Christopher Kroneschmidt, and Corey Attaway.

Other colleagues and friends read the manuscript and listened to my ideas and steadily offered suggestions to sharpen or improve the work. Among them are Henry Pontell, Gil Conchas, Paul Jessilow, and the editors at Waveland Press, especially Jeni Ogilvie. Finally, I want to thank Father Gregory J. Boyle who graciously agreed to write a foreword and whose insights on street youths and dedication to finding a new way to address their problems should serve as a beacon to the rest of us.

chapter
1

Addressing the
Gang Problem

Since the 1980s, most gang control efforts have been conducted by the police in an after-the-fact manner—after youths have joined a gang. All too often, debate over the correct response to youth gangs has devolved into an either/or response: shape up or go to jail. Police threaten youths hanging out on street corners with arrest unless they disperse. Youths who commit crimes are arrested, prosecuted, and jailed, without any attempt by authorities to understand the root causes underlying the commission of the crime. Jails are filled with youths who have been prosecuted based on suppression tactics that are ineffective for stopping gangs.

The better strategy to address the gang problem is through an open, balanced approach that offers positive activities, outlets, and role models—one that addresses the complex problems of urban youths (although there are youth gangs in rural and suburban areas as well) whose ecological, socioeconomic, sociocultural, and sociopsychological situations make them vulnerable to joining a gang. For a large segment of our youth population, their lives are filled with more "punishments" than "rewards." This imbalance comes not only from law enforcement policies and strained police relations but also from stressed families, overburdened schools, low-self esteem, and the lack of positive role models. We must right this imbalance. We must return to a time when fear of gangs did not consume us, when efforts to stop gangs provided strategies of reason and balance. Nevertheless, with today's cutbacks and elimination of social nets and programs, there is even less resolve to seriously address the roots of the street gang problem.

It is a false belief that there are no inequities and inequalities in our society, that everyone begins life from the same starting line. If that were

1

true, neighborhoods, homes, schools, socializing routines and rhythms, and the goals and means to reach those goals would be the same for everyone. Instead, tremendous gaps exist between the fortunate and less-fortunate members of our society.

The gang subcultural process unfolds in like manner from place to place—not only in the United States but in other nations as well. To understand this subcultural process as it occurs in Los Angeles gives us valuable insights into this global phenomenon (Hagedorn 2008).

Need for a Balanced Strategy

What is needed today to address gang problems (and other social problems as well) is a balanced strategy of prevention, intervention, and law enforcement. We must reproduce a carrot-and-stick—reward and punishment—approach in a way that enables millions of parents to help their children follow a conventional life. Our children deserve opportunities and choices early in life that provide rewards in order to steer them in a productive direction.

An example of why we need a new approach is found in a *Los Angeles Times* (Spano 2007) article on the apprehension and arrest of a new group of gang members. These members were intimidating residents of a neighborhood and controlling the drug trafficking there. FBI officials stated that this new group had filled the void left by another group eliminated six years before in an anti-gang sweep. The way this earlier incident played out reinforces what I wrote many years ago: "After the sheriffs conducted a sweep of Barrio Cuca in 1978, arresting and jailing a number of very active gang members, the community remained fairly quiet for a couple of years. However, since the sheriffs took only one cohort away, it was only a matter of time before a new cohort surfaced. When it did, the barrio street life would be rekindled." The lesson here is that the solution to gangs is not found in jailing each new cohort. "We seem to forget that urban youth gangs have plagued America since the turn of the [20th] century. . . . As long as certain environmental and economic patterns persist, the gang subculture will continue to recruit new members" (Vigil 1988a: 174–175). The situations and conditions that created the gang and gang members in the first place still have not been adequately addressed.

Currently in Los Angeles there are two anti-gang legal channels available to combat gangs: STEP (Street Terrorism Enforcement and Prevention Act) and the Gang Injunction. STEP is a special law that adds enhancements in penalties for any gang member who is charged with a crime. The legal definition in this law of who is a gang member has been cobbled together by public lawyers, not by researchers who have studied gangs. Moreover, opinions even in this latter group vary tremendously in what constitutes a gang and a gang member. Thus, the application of STEP to gang members has been inconsistent and widely misapplied by police officials and prosecutors.

The Gang Injunction, in contrast, is a practice that attempts to break up the gang by following a legal path that leads to a judge filing an "injunction" that bars gang members who live in a named gang neighborhood from hanging around together. Each of the known members of the gang is also named and is served a court document that informs him or her of this ruling and the legal consequences if the gang member defies or breaks it. Besides major problems in determining who is on the list, whether they are still active gang members, and how they might avoid this designation, there is a far more glaring problem associated with this draconian legal statute. According to the rationale of this law, it is supposed to target gangs that are the most violent and troublesome, those that are a public nuisance. Yet, research shows that it in fact focuses on gangs that are close to middle-class neighborhoods or areas that are being gentrified (Alonso 1999, 2010).

Multiple Marginality

Street gangs in the United States, and probably elsewhere, are the result of marginalization, that is, the relegation of certain persons or groups to the fringes of society, where social and economic conditions result in powerlessness (Hazlehurst and Hazlehurst 1998; Szanton Blanc et al. 1995; Vigil 1987). It is a process that begins with where people live and raise their families; what type of work and status they've attained; how place and status, in turn, shape the patterns of parenting, schooling, and policing; and finally, the personal and group identities that emerge in this marginalized context. A broad linking and sequencing of these features show the additive and cumulative nature of the emergence of gangs and the generation of gang members.

One starting point for understanding the initial stage of marginalization is to examine the processes and situations of immigration. America's long gang history began in the mid-nineteenth century when ethnically distinct populations, Irish and Italians especially, came to this country. At that time, children of immigrant parents were particularly affected as they struggled to adapt to a new culture and life, thus distancing themselves from their parents' lifeways. Meanwhile, their parents had to find jobs for themselves and a way to raise their families in an urban setting, another unsettling situation, especially since they came

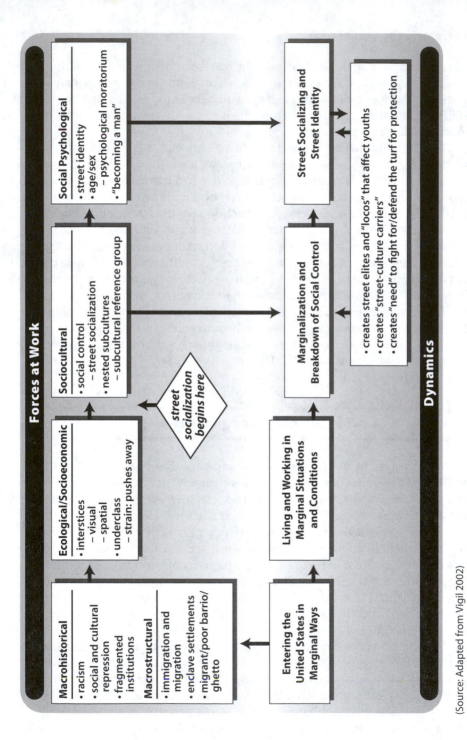

Forces at Work

Macrohistorical
- racism
- social and cultural repression
- fragmented institutions

Macrostructural
- immigration and migration
- enclave settlements
- migrant/poor barrio/ghetto

Ecological/Socioeconomic
- interstices
  - visual
  - spatial
- underclass
  - strain: pushes away

Sociocultural
- social control
  - street socialization
  - nested subcultures
  - subcultural reference group

Social Psychological
- street identity
- age/sex
  - psychological moratorium
- "becoming a man"

street socialization begins here

Dynamics

Entering the United States in Marginal Ways

Living and Working in Marginal Situations and Conditions

Marginalization and Breakdown of Social Control

Street Socializing and Street Identity

- creates street elites and "locos" that affect youths
- creates "street-culture carriers"
- creates "need" to fight for/defend the turf for protection

(Source: Adapted from Vigil 2002)

Framework of multiple marginality: "act and react"

mostly from small, rural environs where conditions were different. Today, many immigrants come from the southern section of the Western Hemisphere and experience the same challenges past immigrants faced.

The process of adaptation, experienced by both past and current immigrants, affects family structure and stability, schooling readiness in the context of language and cultural differences, and points of contact with police and the criminal justice system. It is a process, as we will note, that unfolds on many levels as a product of pressures and forces in play over a long period of time. In short, the phrase "multiple marginality" reflects the complexities and persistence of these forces. As a theory-building framework, multiple marginality encompasses ecological, economic, sociocultural, and psychological factors that affect adaptation and underlie street gangs and youths' participation in them (Covey, Menard, and Franzese 1992; Vigil 1988a, 1988b, 2002). The effects of multiple marginality's social control also lead to gang formations.

This book begins by describing how poverty and marginalization lead to "street socialization" (i.e., a cohort of youth being raised in the streets) and the emergence of street gangs and gang members. It continues with how social control breakdowns and human development processes are undermined and revamped by stressful and difficult situations and conditions that seem hopeless. Specific examples of new ways to address these destructive and detrimental events and episodes are offered to give readers a better idea of how a strategy that integrates prevention and intervention approaches with those of suppression can be successful. The account uses a time, place, and people foundation: ways to "steal" time

A crumbling neighborhood walkway

(e.g., fill voids in family life) using "timely" (age appropriate) interventions; change the pressures and demands of place (the home and the street); and introduce a new supporting cast of people to guide and supervise the urban children most prone to the pull of street socialization.

Street Socialization

Socialization is the process by which a person learns the way of a given social group and is molded into an effective participant. Street socialization is an aspect of the barrio (and other ethnic enclaves) that undergirds established gangs and is conducted, to a considerable degree, away from home, school, and other traditional institutions. The most multiply marginal youths are often the most unsupervised and reside in crowded housing conditions where private space is limited. These youngsters are driven into the public space of the streets where peers and teenaged males, with whom they must contend, dominate. These peers and older males provide a new social network and models for new normative behavior, values, and attitudes. They also make youngsters feel protected from other combative gang members who pose a possible threat.

Thus, because of the *situations* (e.g., exposure only to run-down and spatially separate enclaves; lack of or limited access to and identity with dominant institutions; social and cultural conflicts between first- and second–generation family members; and so on) and *conditions* (e.g., inferior, crowded housing; low or inadequate income; and so on), many urban youths are compelled to seek the dynamics of the street.

One of the first goals in the streets is to determine where one fits in the hierarchy of dominance and aggression that are required for survival. Being from a family that has gang members—a brother, uncle, or other relative—helps in gaining entrance into the gang and additionally offers generational continuity for the gang itself. Otherwise, a young new member gets protection by seeking out associates who are street wise and experienced and willing to be friends. In turn, this prompts the youth to return the favor by thinking and acting in ways approved by his friends. In this way, the newly established social bonds are reinforced, a sense of protection is gained, and new behavior patterns and values are learned. In short, most street-raised youths must come to terms with the cohort of their barrio who controls the streets.

The streets also provide youths with opportunities for adventure and—in the absence of effective adult supervision—with the freedom to undertake those adventures. A boy can wander where he will and return when he wishes, answering to no one or, at worst, facing a spanking or berating from his often absent parents when he returns home. In this aura of freedom, other children are now one's reference group, and their values and guidelines encourage activities outside the limits of adult approval. Experimentation with alcohol and drugs occurs, weapons are

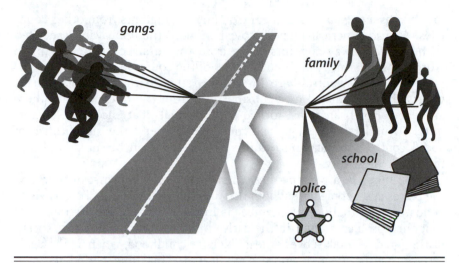

Multiple marginality's effects on social control

accepted as the equalizer when needed, deviant actions are taken on a dare, and bonds with similarly street-active peers who are also school classmates are intensified.

Much of this preteen interaction provides the fertile ground for later teen-year bonding when more serious gang affairs are introduced. Many of the incidents exhibiting protection, daring, managing fear, and conducting mischievous acts are seared into the memories of such youths. The remembrance of things past is often the basis for instilling loyalty and comrade-in-arms friendships that make later gang affiliations so strong and immutable. Street socialization thus becomes the basis for entrance into the gang and the preservation of the gang lore and traditions. It is the first phase of the integration into the gang subculture that for some individuals is a steady, uninterrupted development.

Breakdowns in Social Control and Gang Subcultures

Society, through its social control institutions, is intent on making sure its citizens behave in acceptable ways and defines the proper action to take when they don't. As anthropologists have long noted, social control is an important function of all cultures, one in which the family universally plays a key role. When family or other normative social forces and influences do not function as they should, street subcultures arise to fill the void. The structure and form of the family and other institutions of social control vary from society to society, and more so in the case of immigrant families. With these families the disruptions and marginalization they face in moving from one society to another greatly affects them. The new place, in large part, determines how successfully the family can function as an agent of social control. Like immigrants from other countries, African Americans have also experienced the upheavals associated with adaptation, as migrants come from the rural South to the urban North—two distinctly different regions of the country.

Some social controls are internalized (i.e., within the individual), others are externalized mechanisms (i.e., from the outside), and there are also various sanctions, formal and informal, that encourage conformity. To understand gangs one must comprehend the significance of social control ramifications, as this broad issue can be integrated into multiple marginality.

The times in a person's life when these street processes occur, and the places and people with whom they unfold, are important because they almost predict that a gang member is in the making. Family strains and schooling problems erupt in the early childhood years, and street socialization gradually takes over at least by later childhood; when adolescence arrives, matters become more complicated. This time period leads to associations with a multiple-aged peer group of the streets that eventually dominates in the acquisition and retention of values and norms that contrast markedly with those accepted by the dominant society. Such social control breakdowns completely transform and undermine human development trajectories that affect cognitive, physical, social, and emotional needs and desires (this will be discussed later in the chapter).

Integral to the social control breakdown are the isolation and detachment from other communities that make the barrio gang members wary of outsiders. Threats and challenges directed at one member are taken seriously by the entire gang; an infraction against one member is an affront to all. Defense of turf is a *raison d'être* for a barrio gang and a subcultural solution to feeling marked as fair game. The bonds of mutual trust based on friendships encourage gang membership and participation for protection. Within certain areas of southern California, there exist numerous barrios, some of the classic type and others more loosely defined, that have for decades been "at war" with one another. This conflict tradition is passed on through the generations. Most youths who join a gang, and even most who do not, know who the enemies are and how to fight them. An awareness and identification with the gang is facilitated by the customary way that past events and incidents are remembered and recalled, as a type of oral history, to build up the image and reputation of the barrio gang. Lore, legend, and even myth with specially "embossed" stories, are the vehicles with which the spoken word has helped the subculture survive. This is certainly a new value system of the streets.

By focusing on these socialization experiences, we can gather facts, describe transformations, and offer interpretations of where family life and its structures unravel, how schools fail, why law enforcement remains disconnected from low-income communities, and when a multiple-aged peer group and street socialization begin to dominate the life of a youth. Only

Parking lot in an alley

when we have command of this information can new prevention, intervention, and suppression approaches be generated and potential fixes debated and contemplated. It is a micro framework (analysis of social control) within a macro framework (multiple marginality) that is parsimonious and focused and lends itself to cross-cultural analysis and policy formation.

Deviance or Conformity?

Perhaps we should take the question most researchers ask and turn it upside down. Instead of asking, Why do youths *deviate* from the values and norms of society?, we should ask, Why do youths *conform* to the values and norms of society? The latter question recognizes that humans are born unsocialized and must learn the rhythms and routines of society and embrace them. They do this by forming bonds with significant persons, teachings, and examples at various times and places, which condition people to operate within the expectations of mainstream society. If societal bonds are weak or nonexistent, the individual is more likely to chart a path away from societal expectations and toward a different set of expectations.

There are connections (family members), engagements (school goals), involvements (time spent with whom? where? when? how?), and beliefs (adherence to central value and normative systems) in the processes of socialization (Vigil 2002).

An individual's connections, or social bonds, with significant others ordinarily begin with the family and gradually extend to others outside kinship networks starting mainly at school. However, multiple marginalization erodes social bonds and contributes to the breakdown of family life and schooling routines, resulting in a generally untethered existence for a youth, which leads to more time spent on the streets. Outside the purview and supervision of adult caretakers (in the home and school specifically), the youth undergoes a socialization influenced and guided by a street-based peer group—the resident gang. This street-based socialization becomes a key factor in developing not only different social bonds but also different aspirations for achievement, levels and intensities of participation, and belief patterns.

Moreover, macrohistorical and macrostructural forces also often undermine the normal attachment processes of many youths who end up in gangs, and these forces often generate shocks that detach family members from each other. Socioeconomic factors such as poverty, economic dislocation, divorce, single-parent households, and racism place severe stresses on many families, so that home life is regularly unstable. Unable to provide adequate sustenance for their children, many parents lose their coping skills entirely and fail to supervise and guide their offspring in the development of their social bonds. When this unstable situation persists for years, an attitude of resignation and defeat gradually develops. Mother-centered households are especially vulnerable, and many gang youths suffer the additional consequences of an absent father.

Human Development Trajectories

Overall, street socialization undermines and transforms the conventional course of human development in ways that institutionalize a street subculture. What are these human developmental themes and how do they unfold under the breakdowns of social control and the onset of street socialization? What follows are some guiding thoughts on this issue. Research evidence points to the early lives of children without supervision who become gang members. As compared to other youths who don't join gangs, gang children have traumatic lives, filled with negative events and episodes that characterize their upbringing (Vigil 1988a, 2002). The gang life path has a whole set of unique roadways, turns, narrow choices, and seductive draws, all of which shape youths' personal and group identity. Ultimately, and as we will note in full detail later, when youths reach the psychosocial moratorium (the onset of puberty), the effects of the ecocultural context of an impoverished area on the growth and maturity of a gang child are clear.

Human development in early childhood (age 5–9 years) entails many physical needs, and if these go unmet then new socialization paths are forged. These youngsters have high energy and activity levels, and they enjoy practicing new skills. In short, they are always moving and experimenting. Unfortunately, the reality of a ghetto or barrio of crowded homes often includes the lack of green space or recreational facilities, so children's movement can be considerably limited to an environment of walled-off spaces, crowded conditions, and pavement. Thus, these children seek areas near their home, usually alleyways and garages, to play. They may even expand their space to places across the street or at the end of the block. When young children are separated and away from the supervisory eyes and ears of adult caretakers, early street socialization occurs.

Along with the physical aspect of child development there is also the cognitive side of the equation. Children learn by actively doing things that are progressively exciting and stimulating. Unless children are involved in regular programs with a set schedule and trained caretakers, the cavorting and participation is a hit or miss affair often away from home and where irregular, spontaneous street flare-ups and disputes dominate—older children bullying or taking toys away, the possibility of adult neighbors or strangers as potential molesters, and temptation for risky, dangerous behavior.

In the social realm, for children ages 5–9 ego formation is just beginning. The striving awareness for a sense of self requires much guidance and attention on a one-on-one basis. Self-confidence is fostered by participating in events and situations that build a sense of personal efficacy. Too often family strains interfere with this need to establish self-confidence. Parents may lack the ability or opportunity to interact with their children themselves or to enroll them in programs in which trained adults can meet children's needs. Thus, the real-life experiences in poverty-stricken gang neighborhoods often entail, even at this early age, playmates and play areas that are happenstance events. Social nooks and crannies are found some distance from home and adults, out of eyesight and earshot in a very unsupervised reality. It is here that older children enter the picture as leaders and bullies—the beginnings of the multiple-aged peer group. In these circumstances, personal feelings are extremely volatile. Reality is so fraught with uncertainties and sometimes danger, the "dramas" of family members or others involved in the child's life dominate the emotional climate and skew developmental pathways.

In later childhood (ages 9–14) physical changes are dramatic as the onset of puberty takes on an bumpy course of its own. There is an even stronger need at this age for positive anchoring experiences to show achievement and for opportunities to shine. How to strive, aspire, and achieve to gain status is a driving force at this age and developmental phase. One must give the physical appearance of control, of mastery over one's life. It is "machismo in motion" because of the adolescent need for gender role clarification. Clearly, Walter Miller's (1958) work on lower-class culture and the need for physical prowess and dominance is relevant here. Fighting and physical strength and appearance help present an image and role of a courageous, brave, aggressive, fearless "man" who would resort to violence if necessary. More elaboration on this life passage event and other gang dynamics follows in subsequent chapters.

Because of hormonal imbalances and the changing nature of social expectations, mental and physical inconsistencies play havoc with the cognitive side of a person during this developmental phase. Earlier childhood habits and social cues are incongruous with a new behavioral environment that shapes and makes other demands. This incongruity, however, is handled rather masterfully by presenting a social front. For the Mexican gang member, it is the *cholo* role, where dress, talk, walk, and demeanor become the street style to emulate and follow. Erikson (1968) once said of this universal phenomenon: "There are uniform ways of doing things (i.e., patterns, norms) and a uniformed way of doing it (dress, physical appearance)" (p. 63). This front assuages deeply perceived changes in expectations. It is a cardboard image that trumps all the human development tensions, helping merge ego, group, and role all in one swoop.

Social and emotional development, as expected for this age group, becomes more peer dependent, and the intensity of relationships increases. The desire to be well liked and surrounded by friends, free from adult supervision, is part of the autonomy that many preadults strive for. Unusual though this sounds, however, in most cases of street socialization, friends and bonds are already established by this age. Street-socialized adolescents have learned quite early which people to befriend and whom they want to like them; often it is the street icons— the *veteranos* (veterans) or OGs (original gangsters) whom they look up to and aspire to emulate.

Street bonding episodes can run the gamut from criminal adventures far from home to petty capers, such as shoplifting or stealing something, close to home. Even though these youths are more self-conscious on the road to personhood, they regularly display a sense of independence in front of observers. It is a difficult balancing act; they seek a place that will give them a safe autonomy but also want links to emotionally supportive networks. However, in the street scene for gang members, which they have already been socialized to, there is more pressure to adopt the street image necessary for networks of survival. It makes sense, in the twisted, torqued way of the streets, to surrender independence or autonomy once the group syndrome dominates all else.

A Balanced Strategy Based on Root Causes

We now look at how prevention, intervention, and suppression approaches can be generated from the breakdowns of social control, their replacement by street socialization, and the disruption of conventional human development trajectories. A macrohistorical look at today's gang problem would reveal that race and racism are continuing factors along with fragmented cultures and isolated enclaves in characterizing gang communities. In addition, macrostructural forces still plague the access to and acquisition of material resources, housing and health care needs, and the overall well-being of these populations. We must examine gang roots through the prism of the historical and structural experiences of ethnic minority youth. From there, establishing the factual basis of time, place, and people will inform the formulation and implementation of anti-gang strategies.

Los Angeles is both a model of urban diversity, full of different languages and cultural traditions, and a potential tinderbox of ethnic and racial tensions. The history of Los Angeles features rapid and uneven change that brought untold consequences to the low-income and ethnic minority communities. During this metamorphosis, both internal migration (from small towns and various regions of the country) and large-scale immigration (from foreign countries) increased exponentially, eventually pushing white working- and middle-class residents into the suburbs.

One can imagine the social transformations under these continuing situations and conditions, where family life was strained to the point that parents' coping skills were lost and a segment of youths was unleashed from adult influences. The city's infrastructure and institutional support systems were unable to stem the tide. Affordable housing became a problem for many, first in low-income areas like Watts and much later in older, once prosperous neighborhoods like Pico-Union, where Central

Rousting gang members
in the projects

Americans made their home. Both homes and schools were filled to beyond capacity. Schools built for several hundred students were expected to hold twice that number. For decades, as African American and Chicano leaders railed against unfair and unequal treatment of the people in the mostly low-income communities they represented, police–community relations also took a turn for the worse.

Under these circumstances human development became contaminated, as voids and missteps accrued so quickly that a once easy to solve wayward-children problem metastasized into a deeply rooted gang subculture with values and rules of its own. Essential cognitive, physical, social, and emotional changes in children's growth were incomplete or turned on their back. The comprehensive anti-gang strategy presented in this book should help break down the artificial barriers that warring domestic political ideologies have constructed, which often present us with a false choice in dealing with street youth—a choice between coercion and surrender. I have considered these issues over decades, and it always struck me as ironic how ideology can create disconnects that hinder problem solving.

chapter 2

The Roots
of Gangs

The brief summaries in chapter 1 offered key factors in the rise and persistence of street gangs, and we now elaborate and clarify certain points to fully ground the basis for a balanced gang strategy. We first focus on adolescence and the middle school—when gangs begin to strongly influence youths—and then provide systematic explanations of human development changes and gang characteristics that any anti-gang strategy must consider.

Where It All Comes into Focus: Middle School

Once ties with authorities—that is, family, schools, and police— become problematic, conditions are set for the gang to become a substitute surrogate authority that parents, schools, and polices its own members. The modeling and mimicry that occur on the streets become more formalized in the pre- and early teenage years, usually when youths are in middle school (which can include youths anywhere from 12 to16 years old), when the adolescent status crisis results in new experimentation. The transition to middle school means that youths must encounter and react to a new environment and group of students from other neighborhoods or barrios, setting in motion other events. While adjusting to the different demands of middle-school schedules and teacher expectations, the middle-school student must also cope with the various groups and cliques that have carved out niches. Gangs are already evident at this level, and the schoolyard has its separate barrios—gang hangouts where the youngsters gravitate. Ready-made friends and protectors are there, some of whom the newcomers already know, while others are strangers; as noted below, there is an initiation ordeal awaiting the newcomers. In elementary school, they may have heard about these other barrio groups and are thus prepared for them, but seeing them for the first time provides an impetus for their own gang affirmation. While some individuals might have participated earlier in conflicts with rival barrios, and all are aware of such deeply rooted contentions, most youths encounter the hostilities and antagonisms for the first time in the middle-school setting.

Hanging with the homeboys

Early conflicts at school are not too serious, involving mostly challenging looks and stare downs, pushing, and crowding someone's space. Occasionally, an arranged time and place are set after school for two rival individuals to meet and fight. Sometimes such an incident escalates, resulting in serious harm to a participant. More serious conflicts between barrios are directed by the older teenagers and veteranos who have unresolved and continuing rivalries of their own; they often bring in the younger members to help them. The latter are eager to do so, but they still maintain their own rivalries at school and in the neighborhood.

As conflicts increase and intensify at middle school, an individual's reputation spreads as a known and committed gang member. This can especially create problems for a cholo (i.e., from the Spanish word solo, a marginal person) newcomer whose parents have recently moved into the area. Even though he might not be affiliated with the established gangs of the area, he still presents himself as a cholo (e.g., with dress style and mannerisms) and thus is an inferred gang member.

For age and sex clarifications, one is taught to think and act mature and responsible around other gang members, even if it requires antisocial activities like fighting, using drugs and/or alcohol, and opposing school and other authorities. Since many of these youths' households are mother centered, without consistent adult male supervision, the male-dominated street socialization encourages supermasculine behavior. In middle school the early and continuing street pressures generate a strong need to "act like a man," as defined by the gang and demonstrated by the living example of former gang members. Youths are expected to show aggression and test their manhood under the group-patterned auspices of the gang.

To aid in this adolescent adjustment, the gang has developed a cohorting, or cliquing, tradition. For example, El Hoyo Maravilla, White Fence, and Cuatro Flats, three long-standing classic barrios, have each generated a succession of separate age-graded cliques since their inception (see Moore 1978; Vigil 2007:66). Such barrios always have at least two or three cohorts defined by age and status (and sometimes more, if some members are unable or refuse to "mature out" of the gang). There are the 12–16-year-olds in middle school, who are just getting into the gang; the 14–18-year-olds in high school (or who have dropped out), who are somewhat proven; and the 18–20-year-olds who are seasoned. In addition there are the veteranos, who are in their middle or late 20s or even in their 30s, who play a role as titular leaders and models, sages of the street, of sorts. This age grading, with its informal and formal processes of socialization and enculturation, ensures that the barrio gang always has a new clique to take over the duties of defending the turf.

Initiation into this way of thinking and acting has usually been formalized as a rite of passage. If not earlier, by middle high school a prospective gang member is initiated into the gang by being "jumped in"— that is, surrounded and beaten by two, three, or more other gang members. This ordeal is a type of street ceremony, or baptism, that confirms how interested the novitiate is in joining the gang and also provides an opportunity for older gang members to assess the potency of the new member whom they *are allowing* into the gang (Vigil 1996).

To summarize, middle school is the social arena where major gang involvement and behavior occurs. Aiding this transition, of course, is the adolescent tendency to seek peers for guidance and direction in fashioning a new identity. The middle school environment adds an important dimension—the presence of other barrio gangs that provide an external force or threat to hasten gang affiliation. With initiation and the integration of the signs and symbols of the cholo, the youngster experiments with more serious gang patterns, such as conflicts with other gangs, and is on his way to dedicating his life to *mi barrio* (my neighborhood), a type of surrender of self to the group.

How Marginalization and Street Socialization Affect Human Development

As previously noted, in the wake of marginalization, the street socialization process affects several features of the lives of gang members, mainly those stemming from the voids in their home and school experiences. To fill these voids, youngsters find their way out into the streets, the alleyways, rooftops, empty lots, and street corners. What starts off as play groups, initially merely mischievous and adventurous, ends up evolving into a local street gang subculture with its own rules and regulations. In time, a multiple-aged peer group makes up the gang. The end result is a street population bereft of conventional socialization influences from home, school, and law enforcement, and because no one stepped in, a street gang has evolved into a quasi-institutionalized youth subculture where older males help guide and induct the novitiates into street gang ways. Street gangs have always been conducive to street crimes, but for decades that was not central to their reason for being. Now, however, it is becoming more common for some of these gang members to slip into association with organized crime, such as the drug cartels that dot the Mexican–U.S. border or other larger hemispheric networks.

Human developmental processes, as is to be expected, are considerably altered and undermined under marginalization and street socialization circumstances. The obstacles and barriers (the punishments!) often dwarf reward options. Even though these conditions affect all youths in these places, it is the poorest of the poor and most culturally conflicted individuals and groups that are hardest hit. It is they who are most prone to "deep" street socialization and becoming gang members, that is, spending more time in places with other people who are antisocial and deviant.

Although all the youths are stressed by the environment of multiple marginalization, only about 10 to 15 percent of youths in most of these neighborhoods formally join gangs (Esbensen & Winfree 2001; Short 2001; Vigil 1988a). The other 85–90 percent are less marginal on most of the social, economic, and cultural dimensions mentioned above and thus more apt to follow a conventional path (see Vigil 2007:85). Of the 10–15 percent of youths who choose gang life, about 70 percent "mature out" (Vigil 2007). Within the more vulnerable population, various aspects of human development—social, emotional, cognitive, and physical realms—

Stoop culture

show when and where youths made their choices, or, more correctly, what conditions compelled them into street socialization and thus an unconventional life path. Understanding these decision trees illuminates what is to follow.

The Social Realm

First, there is the desire to belong, both for protection and for social reasons. It is fairly obvious that the social dimension of the gang is perhaps its most important one. The "desire to be well liked" is common across most adolescent groups, but this human aspiration takes different turns and twists among gang members. It is within a street-based arena that the judgment is made as to being liked, and with whom and for what reason. In the absence of conventional influences, the caretakers and teachers who guide youths through these "mean streets" end up being the older gang members—the most significant players of the multiple-aged peer group. These veteranos or OGs are the power brokers of the street with whom everyone must contend, including youths who are nongang members. Veteranos are both feared as potential predators and respected as potential protectors. Much of the gang behavior of youths stems from this fear, and they tend to emulate those whom they fear most while simultaneously seeking protection from them. But even more, the older gang member represents power—for a youth seeking to mold his self-image, this is someone who would be good to be liked and accepted by.

The Emotional Realm

The second category, the emotional realm, features the crisis passage into puberty, which entails bodily changes and hormonal adjustments and imbalances. For all youth, making the passage from childhood to adulthood involves a marginal status crisis known as the *psychosocial moratorium*, which is a time when adolescents experiment with new roles and often tend to avoid or strongly dismiss traditional adult supervision. There is a heightened sense of personal ambiguity and confusion that affects self-identification pathways, with these developments becoming more self-conscious in the context of street life where pressures and demands are sometimes overwhelming (Erikson 1968; Vigil 1988a, 1988b, 2002).

According to Erikson (1968) the psychosocial moratorium is the marginal status crisis of adolescence in the passage from childhood to adulthood. It is arguably the most pivotal episode in the lives of budding gang members. It can be a life-turning event to help cement them to the rhythms and routines of the street or it could be a passing brush with the gang lifestyle. Street males in low-income neighborhoods are especially affected by the transition as they become tentative and confused about their age and gender identity. The personal and psychological struggle that occurs in this context is sometimes overwhelming. This "storm and stress" situation triggers many attitudinal and behavioral shifts that make individuals unpredictable and ambivalent. Being raised in the streets can make this human development phase more difficult and problematic, twisting and skewing options and opportunities in ways that are detrimental.

Ego formation, group affiliation, and adoption of role behavior dominate during this time. This is especially the case because there is developmental tension between early household socialization, often dominated by females, and the new street socialization under the aegis of the male multiple-aged peer group. It is no mere coincidence that it is youths ages 12–16 years who experience the most personal tension and conflict and who are more apt to run afoul of the law (Hirschi and Gottfredson 1983). At this stage of life, egos are fragile, misshapen, or fragmented. How the ego is shaped and grows determines if there is an overreliance on the group, in which case the person becomes peer-dependent and surrenders to the group.

The Cognitive Realm

The need for friends to like you and relying on them almost exclusively for guidance and direction can also play havoc at the cognitive level. In this developmental level, certain incongruous behaviors—trying to act tough when one is not, overdressing in the street style, not carrying school books home, playing to the gang audience, and faking defiance of authorities—give individuals a positive feeling about themselves. In keeping with this variable behavior, some gang members portray an almost Jekyll and Hyde character, reflecting a chameleon aspect of gang life.

The Physical Realm

Much of what was said about the emotional state of the mind during puberty applies to the final human development feature, physical changes. While the interior of a person is undergoing mostly masked changes, it is much more obvious when physical appearance makes a statement about ambiguity and uncertainty. Voice changes, increases in height, and bodily alterations remake the person and place the control and management of one's self-image under siege.

Voices are feigned to evince a deeper masculine sound, body muscles are strained and enlarged to give the appearance of strength and physicality, and a slow and methodical movement style strikes a pose that someone is in control and knows how to manage any situation. All through this uneven posturing is the inner-child struggling to make a statement on how successful or competent a youth is or should be. However, in contrast to dominant-society teenagers who are socialized in conventional areas of accomplishment, the streets have dictated a different arena. It is obvious that showing strength and hardiness helps in street-life survival, and some individuals come from harshly abusive lives, which makes them even tougher. Some are even out of control, in a rage, mad at the world and getting even with anyone and everyone.

Veteranos waiting for a job

Physical transformations send a message to onlookers: here is a person who is a work in progress. Responding to this transformation, a youth often needs to show mastery by achieving or shining in some capacity.

Fighting Fear, Managing "Toughness"

In contrast to teenagers who are socialized in conventional areas of accomplishment, street youths demonstrate their prowess in a different arena. First and foremost is showing "toughness." A few actually are very tough, even "out of control"—that is, they can dish it out and they can take it. These individuals are usually the ones who have experienced early childhood traumas or are unsure of themselves and overdramatize this toughness. A street world shapes a protective physical appearance, a posturing that can serve both to deter potential aggressors and to intimidate—a "street camouflage," so to speak.

On the other hand, many more street youths are often tentative and uneasy about how they demonstrate and manage this toughness. This is especially so for those who are lagging in all or most of the developmental categories. Lacking assurance on how to effect the sought-after image and behavior, and not particularly predisposed to the street culture by early emotional setbacks that would instill a sense of rage, these youths have trouble pulling off the tough posture; for them it is shakily demonstrated and the image comes off more as a blurred, muffled pose. However, for those who succeed in attaining this image, whether they are really tough or faking it, the reward is the admiration of fellow gang members and especially the street community in general.

Monster Kody (Shakur 1993), in his autobiographic account of his street experiences in South Central Los Angeles, describes how you achieve the level of Ghetto Hero from all parties concerned. Once you gain respect and status, you can strut the neighborhood with your head held high. (The drawback, of course, is that like the gunslingers of the Old West, the high level you've achieved may also mark you for others to gain status by knocking you off your perch.) The achievement can also have other benefits. Although many youths use their physical strength and image to gain respect and status among their peers and rival gangs, others leverage their "tough" reputations into careers as drug bosses or gang organizers. They are the "shot callers" who determine when violence is initiated, by whom, and against which rival gang.

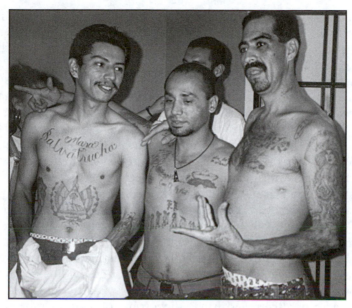

Homies Unidos: members of MS 13 and 18th Street

Locura: Situational or Real?

One role and role performance especially instrumental in the context of street reality is *locura*. It is both essential for street survival and for assuaging fear and ambiguity born of the psychosocial moratorium. Locura is a state of mind where various quasicontrolled actions denoting a type of craziness or wildness occur. A person who is a loco demonstrates this state of mind by alternately displaying fearlessness, toughness, daring, and other unpredictable forms of destructive behavior, such as getting "loco" on drugs and alcohol or excelling in gangbanging. Such traits are, more or less, considered as gang ideals. Some confirmed *vato locos* (crazy gangsters) can easily and authoritatively manage this role, while others only rise to the occasion when peer pressure or situational circumstances dictate a loco act. This difference reflects the distinction Edgerton (1978) makes between deviant persons and deviant acts.

This psychosocial role has become a requisite for street survival and a behavioral standard for identification and emulation; it can also be a quick fix for youths who have not yet attained the strength or physical prowess for displaying toughness. A person who is loco, either situationally or regularly, adds an important dimension to the group. This is especially the case where the barrio is beleaguered by other barrio gangs and must show a stronger force of resistance to outside challenges and pressures. The loco is a prized member of the group for he can sometimes act as a deterrent to stave off confrontations. In many other instances, however, the loco can be a hindrance or detriment to the group when his unbridled actions cause unnecessary and unwanted trouble.

Factors that can be traced directly to the streets, then, are especially important in this regard. One is how a person early on in life has been socialized in the streets, the socialization of last resort when home, school, and other caretakers fail, and thus takes on this crazy persona as an actor. The other one is much more nuanced, unpredictable, and variable. When a person enters the streets later in life, often only temporarily, that person must learn to act like a street person, including acting crazy; that is one reason why drugs and alcohol are used to ease the performance. In short, early painful experiences and/or early street socialization are more likely to result in a crazy actor, while late street socialization is apt to turn out individuals who periodically perform crazy acts. Police most often care little for these distinctions and care about who crosses the line rather than why or how often the line is traversed.

However, Klein (1971, 1995) and others (Cartwright et al. 1975) have noted a hard-core and fringe dichotomy of gang membership, and Klein (1995) has even developed a typology of gangs, as has this author, in distinguishing gang members as regular, peripheral, temporary, and situational. Such typologies reflect differing intensities and durations of gang member involvement and attachment (Vigil 1988a). In brief, there is a tremendous range of locura behavior among individuals within a barrio and between barrios Although these situations and conditions generally affect most gang members, it is the role models with tarnished early lives and street experiences, who most influence the fringe gang members.

What needs to be fathomed is how most caretakers have failed our youth—families and schools primarily—and in the voids left by these institutions, street socialization has taken over to create a basis for a new set of values and norms. In the most marginalized and impoverished communities, for some individuals, a series of personal traumatic experiences and influences have generated a sense of rage and aggression such that lashing out violently becomes a generally predictable and expected type of behavior. In this context of social determinants and psychological propensities, street gangs have become a street-created medium and vehicle to encourage and vent this aggression. Gang case history data gathered over many decades (Vigil 1988a, 2002, 2007) are interpreted within gang literature to provide insights into why we have violent gang actors and why there are individuals who commit violent gang acts—again, the difference between an actor who is loco (crazy) and one who commits a crazy loco act.

Acts or actors, does it make a difference? The Los Angeles gang homicides that reached record levels in 1994 gradually declined in the late 1990s. Only recently have they begun to climb again. Both liberals and conservatives claimed credit for this drop. Liberals pointed to an increase in jobs and social programs under the Clinton administration, whereas conservatives underscored how previously instituted harsher penalties and longer sentences were now showing results. Putting aside the question of jobs or training programs versus more time in jail, the major point is that there were much less violent (crazy) incidents, either episodic acts or endemic actors. If it is true, as I suggest here, that gang members come in different stripes and persuasions, then it follows that knowledge of their backgrounds is essential to understanding their level of locura, real or feigned. This background information better enables us to assess the role performance and enactments that play into gang conflicts and the locura binges that sometimes get out of hand.

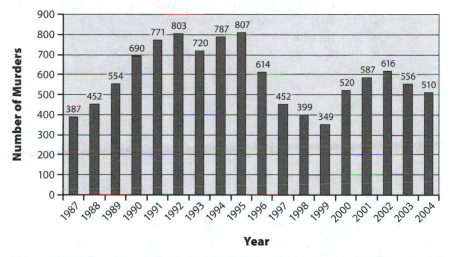

(Source: Adapted from data provided by Sgt. Wes McBride, retired, Los Angeles Sheriff Department)

Gang-related homicides

Human Development Reconsidered

Most adolescent youths have the same basic needs and indulge in many normal or experimental activities, such as striving for friendship, being involved in social gatherings, participating in the daily gossip of their cohort, and even drinking alcoholic beverages and taking drugs. However, youths socialized in the streets face certain obstacles not usually found in areas in which youths rely on families and teachers for their socialization. These obstacles dictate various options that twist and skew such phases and normal activities.

In gang-ridden neighborhoods, the street gang has become a competitor to other sources of identity formation, often replacing family, school, and other conventional influences. Since their modern inception more than six decades ago, street gangs have been made up primarily of groups of male adolescents and youths who have grown up together as children, usually as cohorts in a low-income neighborhood of a city. Those who do so participate together in both conventional and antisocial behavior (Thornberry 2001). The antisocial behavior, of course, attracts the attention of authorities as well as the general public (Bursik & Grasmick 1995; Curry, Richard, & Fox 1994; Decker & Van Winkle 1996).

As a result of street socialization developments and the status crisis of the psychosocial moratorium, street gang violence in Los Angeles has become a central concern of law enforcement authorities. There are many ways to look at and address as well as to analyze gang violence. Most important to an assessment are the social situations and conditions that engender a violent tendency and the personal experiences and motivations that create and mold individuals to carry out these acts.

Solutions Are in the Roots of the Street Gang

What has emerged in this brief outline of the roots and traditions of the street gang lifestyle is that the facts of time, place, and people can serve as a template for a balanced strategy. A balanced strategy to combat gangs would emphasize prevention and intervention. This concerted effort would fill a major contemporary void by adding rewards to the punishments. Taking this broader, more inclusive approach to improving community health by focusing on at-risk youths would also address human developmental processes (social, emotional, cognitive, and physical). Our society must address the problems associated with gang families and re-equip parents with coping strategies to guide their children. Schools are under siege, but we must somehow undertake a serious effort to remediate the educational problems of children at risk.

Prevention must begin in the early childhood years and continue up to age eight or nine. Communities and agencies must take a proactive approach in addressing the primary problems of the general population in low-income areas, as well as factor in secondary prevention for specific at-risk youths and any related issues. Interventions are aimed at the crucial preteen years, from about age 9 to 12 or 13, and should involve treatment and work with youths who are close to but not yet deeply connected to the streets. Dissuading youths early on from the attitudes and behavior that clearly lead to delinquent and criminal paths opens the possibility of a return to more prosocial activities.

Lacking in many of these youths' lives are the pre-employment experiences that assist human growth and development, such as beliefs and behavioral traits reflecting discipline, obedience, punctuality, responsibility, and value and honor in work. It is for this reason that many observers and writers have emphasized that economic concerns matter most in getting youths off the streets—through training, jobs, and other positive endeavors—by engaging them in productive, conventional activities and grounding them in the skills, knowledge, and attitudes that will stay with them for life. This will give them a stake in society. First, though, we need to figure out how to "steal their time" so that they are free to become involved in conventional activities.

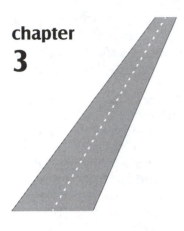

chapter
3

Programs
that Work

The need to examine specific groups, communities, and public institutions in addressing and resolving the gang problem is a well-understood fact. In this chapter, I will elaborate in detail on prevention, intervention, and suppression programs that I have evaluated. The *prevention* program Light of the Cambodian Family targeted the Cambodian community in Long Beach in two schools that worked with five year olds and their parents. All low-income urban neighborhoods can benefit from *intervention* programs, and the one examined here was the Inner-City Games. *Suppression* programs, like prevention and intervention programs, are variable and can be either "soft" or "hard." The one evaluated in this chapter, Community Oriented Policing, is a tactic of a "soft" quality.

In my own ethnographic studies of youth subcultures and education, my qualitative data and insights are contextualized within a quantitative research strategy. Applied anthropologists evaluating the effectiveness of social and cultural change programs have found it useful, even necessary, to rely heavily on their ethnographic skills to acquire relevant information and insights about those programs and their actual effects. Combining information obtained, for example, by participant observation and intensive interviewing of key informants with more readily quantifiable data from other sources ensures a balanced emic and etic understanding. An emic understanding is based on viewing phenomena through the cultural lens of the people whom the program was intended to serve; it roughly corresponds to what we refer to as an insider point of view. On the other hand, an etic understanding is framed in terms of cross-culturally valid social-scientific paradigms and terminology; in a word, it is objective and referred to as an outsider point of view. Thus, in conducting evaluations of the Light of the Cambodian Family in Long Beach,

Inner-City Games in San Jose, and Community Oriented Policing in southern California I relied on both a strong ethnographic component and objective assessments.

As suggested earlier, different facets of human development arise chronologically, and when something goes amiss the chances of a child becoming street socialized increase the possibility of gang induction. Pinpointing that time period and place where children are in jeopardy is crucial for any intervention effort we can make. We need to redirect them away from gangs and the type of street people that dominate their unconventional socialization. My examination and evaluation of the above programs reflect the different age levels of children and underscore the human development issues, such as physical, cognitive, and social/emotional, that need to be addressed. Later, in subsequent chapters, elaborations of other strategies and programs will be outlined to provide readers with ample insights to formulate their own anti-gang approach that fits their neighborhood and community.

Niña at the sink in preschool

Light of the Cambodian Family (Prevention)

The Southeast Asian Health Project of Long Beach launched the Light of the Cambodian Family initiative in the early 1990s. The program focused on early elementary school children of the Khmer community, an ethnic enclave that was experiencing a serious gang problem with adolescent youths. It was a prevention effort precisely because the target age was six years old, first-graders, and their adult caretakers or parents. The program took into account several of the human development needs, such as how the children released their energy, how they were cared for at home, their self-esteem, and so forth. Efforts focused on measuring progress toward eight objectives set forth in the formal design of the evaluation.

1. To increase self-esteem and social acceptance

2. To improve problem-solving, decision-making, and negotiation skills

3. To increase knowledge of Cambodian (Khmer) language and culture

4. To increase positive classroom behaviors and decrease disruptive behaviors

5. To increase school attendance

6. To increase knowledge of the positive effects of healthy and safe behavior and the negative consequences of alcohol, drugs, gangs/violence

7. To improve parenting skills

8. To increase parents' knowledge of the positive effects of healthy and safe behavior and the negative consequences of alcohol, drugs, and gangs/violence

Children's Instructional Services

Instruments used in assessing children's progress included the Preschool Interpersonal Problem Solving (PIPS) test. The PIPS test measures children's problem-solving skills (important for self-esteem and self-confidence). Additionally, word-picture tests were developed by program staff, including a health-and-safety test to assess awareness of street hazards and unhealthy personal habits and a cultural awareness test aimed at assessing Khmer vocabulary skills and knowledge of Cambodian symbols and customs. The evaluation team also devised a rating instrument for teachers to use in assessing children's classroom behavior. A similar instrument was used in collecting information on the parents' observations of changes in the behavior of their children. School attendance records, as well as interviews of teachers and observations of the cultural awareness classes taught as part of the project, provided data used in evaluating the children's progress.

Children's mean score on the Total Relevant Solutions score from the PIPS test increased significantly after the first year of participation in the program. This improvement indicates improved problem-solving skills (objective 2), which generally correlates with self-esteem and social acceptance (objective 1). The Long Beach public school teachers who have had these children in their first and second grade classes provided supportive evidence of this finding: They reported that the children enrolled in the program increasingly utilized nonaggressive problem-solving in settling problems that arise in the schoolyard.

The children also significantly increased their average performance on both the Cambodian cultural awareness test and the health-and-safety test after the first year of participation. Both the teachers of the Cambodian culture classes and the children's parents who were interviewed by the program's parent liaison worker indicated that most children have continued to show increased knowledge of and interest in Khmer culture.

To prepare for an assessment of children's classroom behavior (objective 4), the evaluation team relied in part on the form devised for teachers to rate children's classroom behavior and how it changed over the course of each year of program participation. The instrument also calls for a rating of children's interactions with one another as they pertain to objectives 1 and 2 and their general academic progress. Teachers for the classes that the children were enrolled in during the school year and subsequent years completed these assessment forms. Their ratings of children's self-esteem, self-acceptance, and problem solving in each year tended to correspond to the results from the PIPS test. Teachers indicated only 1 in 20 students were disruptive in class, and more than 70 percent characteristically participated enthusiastically.

The children participating in the program were all enrolled at one of two elementary schools in Long Beach: Lee and Lincoln. Children participating in the program had slightly higher attendance on average than the general student population at the two schools. In addition to direct measurement and teachers' ratings of children's behavior, the project gathered information on parents' perspectives on the effects of the instructional program on their children. An outreach liaison worker reported that most parents were highly appreciative of the culture enrichment program because children now could express culturally appropriate greetings and show deference to adult relatives and visitors. More than 90 percent of the parents reported their child or children who participated in the program had greatly increased knowledge of Khmer culture as a result of that participation. This belief also included the lessening of intergenerational stress and the strengthening of cultural foundations with moral and ethical values to help deter their children from joining gangs.

Parents' Services

Program strategies related to services for parents have focused on regular meetings of the parents and program personnel, including especially the culture enrichment teachers and the outreach liaison worker. In addition, program personnel and members of the evaluation team participated with parents at traditionally important Cambodian celebrations and American cultural events, including an end of the school-year picnic at which a commencement ceremony was held for children who completed the second year of the culture enrichment program. Parents of more than 90 percent of the student participants joined in celebration.

The liaison worker met individually with and interviewed parents of 52 of the 62 children enrolled in the program. As noted above, over 90 percent of those parents believed the program had significantly improved their children's familiarity with Khmer culture as well as their general comportment. Additionally, most parents indicated that they had gained confidence in dealing with their children, particularly in terms of keeping up with their children's school activities and performance. The culture enrichment teachers noted at the time they were interviewed (near the midway point of the grant period for the program) that over the past several months, in particular, parents had shown increased confidence when they were at parent group meetings held at the schools. They became more familiar with school procedures and more actively sought information about their children's involvement at school; offered advice to program personnel and teachers; and pressed for program changes that they felt would benefit their children.

Perhaps most illustrative of the impact of the program on the parents of student participants were two developments during the school year in which the assessment was conducted. At the beginning of the school year, participating parents petitioned program personnel to enroll some of their older children (beyond the targeted age range and grade levels), in the hope of conveying the same benefits they had observed in their participating children. (A small number of third graders were therefore permitted to attend the culture enrichment classes.) Also, at the picnic mentioned above, at least two Cambodian couples who had come to the park with their neighbors sought out program personnel to plead that their children be admitted to the program; they explained that they desired for their children the benefits they had observed in their participating neighbors' offspring.

Inner-City Games (Intervention)

Beginning in East Los Angeles at the Hollenbeck Youth Center, Inner City Games (ICG) expanded into close to 20 cities across the United States in the late 1990s. My associates and I were asked to conduct a formative evaluation of the ICG after-school program in San Jose, California, where ICG had fashioned a working partnership with the city and other community entities to better address the needs of low-income areas and ethnic minority children. San Jose is an old city of many ethnic enclaves with long-term poverty problems. The general goal of the program is to provide sports, recreational, social, and educational outlets for children ages 8 to 14 years, during March through September, weekdays and Saturdays from 3:00 PM to 8:00 PM.

We visited the program on several occasions and combined survey instruments and observations for our data analysis and determination of the success of the program. The surveys covered personal, family, and demographic information and were administered to hundreds of children participating in such events as computer tutoring, cheerleading, soccer, baseball, crafts, and so on. Observation of the same activities and interviewing children and adults who were in attendance provided additional information that we combined with the survey data. As will presently be noted, the evaluation results were generally positive.

The program used "Mission-Oath-Value" constructs to frame its specific goals, which were to connect youths to the larger world, operate within a coordinated network of other agencies, and help youths say "no" to gangs and drugs.

Overall, the responses of the program participants, parents, and staff in the surveys undertaken by the evaluators were positive. Children enjoyed the activities and the attention that they were given. Staff and other adults were lavish in their positive comments about the program. One major strength of the program is the way the target group, at-risk children for gangs and delinquency, is served and the amount of quality time and care that the staff provided them. Moreover, activities were located in or close to the low-income neighborhoods where the targeted group resided. Nevertheless, even though largely a positive and upbeat intervention from the point of view of participants, parents, and program staff, there were glitches.

No one could deny that the time spent in conventional activities, the places where they took place, and the people that attended to the children were all important elements in creating socialization paths to help negate street socialization. However, many of the objectives featured in the Mission-Oath-Value construct, such as self-respect, determination, courtesy, patience, and responsibility, were irregularly addressed during program activities. While the oaths that the children recited exposed them to principles and values accepted by members of mainstream society, the dissemination and retention of these value constructs needed improvement. For example, "Saying no to gangs, drugs, and violence" is cited in the Mission and Oath preambles and is obviously an important long-term goal of ICG. However, it is difficult to determine if the youths who recited this statement actually lived by it. An independent measurement of this goal would require interviews and/or observations of the children's behavior at home, school, or in their neighborhoods, actions and events that were largely outside the purview of ICG staff.

Clean and Green at work

Another goal of ICG is to work on formulating a comprehensive strategy to build a coordinated, cooperative network among different agencies and entities. The rationale behind this goal is to address the multifaceted needs and problems of the participants of the ICG program. It is in this context that the Mission, Oath, and Value statements and philosophy stand out. Each ICG program has devised its own set of values to fit the populations of its own city, and San Jose has selected appropriate values to emphasize with each program activity. Within these word messages are powerful ingredients for shaping a person's identity. Self-respect, determination, courtesy, patience, responsibility, and the other values are core individual and social qualities that are needed in this world. The theory behind making values a part of the activity is to show how attitudes and behaviors, even in play, are grounded in something concrete with a long-lasting function.

Playing soccer, for instance, means teamwork as well as individual skill, so thinking of others is something to value. Some players have become famous as team players because they provide constant examples that teach a way to think and act that are unselfish and attuned to others. However, just uttering the word, "teamwork," is not enough if the goal is to get children to make the connection between an activity and how they should think and act.

The following are simple points to remember about values. A common anthropological definition is: "a value is something cultural that constitutes the desirable in a system of human action" (Whitten 1996, p. 408). Values can be characterized as the "ought-to's" in life. So if "ought-to's" are what you think you should do (the values), the "blueprints for action" (norms for behavior) show you how to do it. One "ought-to" show *courtesy* to family and friends and act polite, helpful, and respectful when around them. One "ought-to" be *patient* in thought and action and let things take their course. One "ought-to" be *responsible* by carrying one's own weight and by walking the talk. Each of these "ought-to's" is supposed to mold a certain type of behavior. Thus, values and norms, like thoughts and behavior, go together. SELF-RESPECT means to think well of yourself and honor your mind and body. TRUST means to always keep your word and do what you say and mean what you do.

A more simplified explanation of these terms and evidence that the behavior they describe is displayed are necessary if such words-in-action are to be used in the program. Otherwise, there is a hollow ring to the utterances, and their recitation risks becoming a ritual without meaning. We believe that recitation of an oath, like the Pledge of Allegiance, can penetrate the minds and hearts of children if it is simple to understand and if the importance of the words and ritual are emphasized. Moreover, this type of exercise in words and thoughts can lead to practical applications. What follows is how values and norms can connect children to the modern world.

Many of the ICG staff and volunteers, as well as parents, are role models who could themselves be sources that show how the values of play and recreation apply to the wider world. Some aspect of their lives certainly has touched on one of the values, and they may have a life story that could be developed and applied to the world of children in this day and age. In short, the importance of their presence must be emphasized in ways that augment the Mission-Oath-Value objectives. Can some aspect of a volunteer's or a staff member's life story provide an example that relates to the value statement? How about building the play structure around the value tale by giving points or credit to participants who show a cooperative or a teamwork approach? For example, the player who passes the ball more often, who thinks of others, who demonstrates teamwork, and so on can be recognized as the winner. In this way, ICG's philosophy can go beyond the play or activity by reaching for practical, lasting outcomes.

Attitudes, skills, and knowledge (hereafter: ASK) can be acquired or changed in a practical way, and the Mission-Oath-Value component can be the basis for this outcome. Even though ICG emphasizes play and recreation, the values learned and reinforced through these activities can be used as pre-job training and other preparations for life activities, such as handling questions in a job interview with a courteous attitudes and an

Clean and Green staff members gather at a mural

upbeat disposition. In sum, the values that ICG staff teach, demonstrate, and expect form the knowledge base to be resourceful and creative when a situation presents itself. Why not aim the Mission-Oath-Value constructs toward the ultimate goal of working in a job that provides security for self and family, and not the dead-end "McJobs" (e.g., fast food, service, etc.) or roles in the illicit economy that so many inner-city children end up doing?

Among the recommendations to improve upon ICG and help generate reassessments for other such programs are to make interagency contact and communication the highest priority. Part of this initiative would be to establish "hotlines" and safe havens for children that are unsupervised. Mission statements and objectives should be stated and explained early and continue to the end of the activity or lesson. The value oath should be simple to recite and understand and be restated throughout activity sessions. By catching the "vision," the values will be admired, rewarded, internalized, and considered as the "ought-to's" of life.

Community-Oriented
Policing Services (Suppression)

In 2000, the Los Angeles County Sheriff's Department (LASD) Regional Community Policing Institute (RCPI) was organizing and conducting training sessions and workshops throughout the southern California area. The focus of the training was a community and police strategy of problem solving. I was part of an evaluation team brought in to assess and evaluate the structure and effectiveness of the program. The evaluation team provided feedback and insights about the training and technical assistance aspects, and we documented how the program was received by various law enforcement personnel. The training program was a partnership and collaboration with other law enforcement and service organizations in the service area.

An Oversight Committee was established with the representatives of various agencies and other community figures as well as LASD representatives to oversee program goals and objectives. The evaluation team kept the mission goals of the LASD-RCPI in mind during the training and dissemination activities. Team experts and consultants included other professors from nearby colleges and universities, graduate and undergraduate students, and community residents. These research associates and assistants used quantitative and qualitative data-collection methods and analytical procedures in their work. During 2000–2001, a strong ethnographic element was emphasized in the data gathering. This approach was taken in order to provide fuller and deeper interpretations of the activities and interactions associated with the training and dissemination of information.

The mission goals of COPS (Community-Oriented Policing Services) focused especially on establishing a regional information, training, and research facility with three overarching purposes:

1. to conduct training programs on community policing for law enforcement agencies and community partners;

2. to broker relevant community policing resources, community forums, and exchanges and to develop materials and disseminate information to community members, police and/or other government officials, which will provide technical assistance to law enforcement, residents, and community agencies; and

3. to conduct research on the implementation and effects of community policing and collaboration between law enforcement and community agencies.

Pursuant to these goals, the main thrust of the first year's activity was conducting training conferences, seminars, and workshops for law enforcement personnel as well as representatives from community service groups.

Three large area-wide conferences were held during the year in an attempt to provide coverage to the entire region encompassed by the LASD-RCPI program. Topics for the workshops and seminars included: Introduction to Community Policing, Community Policing for Supervisors and Managers, Advanced Criminal/Civil Abatement Workshops, Practical Strategies for Community Mobilization and Partnerships, Crime Prevention Through Environmental Design, Domestic/Family Violence Prevention, Gang Prevention, Community Violence Prevention, and a number of others. Various experts and established trainers from the Sheriff's Department and surrounding law enforcement agencies were engaged as instructors.

Throughout these workshops, especially the large conferences, participant observation of proceedings and interactions formed the basis for qualitative information with which to inform the interpretation of the quantified participants' responses to questions about the training. An additional example of this qualitative perspective was a telephone survey follow-up to the first conference, where short self-report, mostly close-ended survey data was augmented with extensive open-ended survey interviews from a random sample of conference attendees.

The evaluation team sent observers to each of the major training conferences, as well as selected workshops (including all of the sessions provided specifically for the Glendale Police Department, as part of an elaborate case study for evaluation). In addition, interviews were conducted with instructors and with law enforcement and other agency representatives attending the training sessions. Training evaluation forms completed by participants of each conference and/or workshop were also utilized as a source of quantitative and qualitative data in the preparation of specific interim reports. Thus, quantitative information has been mixed with qualitative data to provide the basis for more extensive interpretations and analysis.

These conferences each attracted up to 300 participants, thus accounting for a significant proportion of the close to 2,500 law enforcement personnel and community residents who received LASD-RCPI training during its first year of operations. Two guiding philosophical principles drove the evaluation of the LASD-RCPI's goals and mission. The first entailed an examination and documentation of the program as an experiment in culture change, whereby police culture was to be changed or reorganized in ways to utilize new (or reintroduce old) problem-solving approaches and strategies for combating crime and maintaining order in the community. Second, there was an examination of how the training and dissemination positively affected the acquisition of skills, the rethinking of attitudes, and the assimilation of knowledge. We deduced that the training enabled officers and other law enforcement personnel, once armed with such skills, attitudes, and knowledge base, to carry out their tasks in a community policing framework that simplified and expedited maintaining law and order. Throughout the evaluation we integrated these principles in ways that suggest constructive changes in police culture and improvements in skills, attitudes, and knowledge to gauge effective community policing.

It is abundantly clear that the training and technical assistance provided by the LASD-RCPI was successful at several levels. Attendees at each of the three major conferences, for example, were generally in accord that they learned something of value to aid their policing and law enforcement practices. While the ethnographic assessments of the workshops at each of the conferences highlighted some flaws and weaknesses in subject matter presentation or the style and effectiveness of presenters, there was still general agreement among evaluation team observers that most of the workshops provided useful and constructive information and training. The major advantage of such qualitative insights to these workshops is that immediate verbal feedback to LASD-RCPI supervisors and staff helped generate reconsideration of subject matter and/or presenters for future conference workshops, as well as for the seminars that were held at the main headquarters.

Perhaps the most significant positive outcome of the training is that law enforcement personnel already familiar with and committed to community-oriented policing were empowered in the creation of a "comfort zone" to freely proselytize and speak about the benefits gained from new strategies implemented for maintaining law and order. One officer interviewed in the telephone survey put it in succinct words, "Community policing is real policing and is here to stay."

Among the biggest obstacles to the initiation and implementation of COPS that participants cited, however, is the lukewarm support, even resistance, mounted by middle management at various law enforcement agencies. To address this obstacle, future conferences and training activities of the LASD-RCPI should integrate information and practical tips and underscore the importance of having supervisors and managers leading the way in this venture to change police culture. Overall, it appears that deputies and patrol units are more receptive to change than are their superiors. The LASD-RCPI does conduct advanced workshops aimed at supervisors and managers, but even here there was disgruntlement among the lower ranked managers (sergeants mostly) who voiced complaints about superiors with "run-a-tight-ship" rigidity.

Overall, police culture was challenged by LASD-RCPI activities, prompting many participants to reevaluate current practices, but others, who felt threatened, to become defensive and attempt to legitimize the status quo. In large part, the notion of "risk taking" is not that popular in law enforcement hierarchies specifically and bureaucracies in general. Notwithstanding this entrenched attitude, this aspect of police culture should be squarely confronted. In its stead, training must offer a practical demonstration of how new strategies contribute to a different knowledge base and the acquisition of innovative skills to expedite police work. The central idea to community policing is problem solving. A specific workshop on this subject was well organized and well received when it was presented in larger conferences as well as in smaller workshops. However, the subject matter should be integrated into all the workshops. An area to work on is how to situate problem-solving practical tips in the other workshops that address gangs, domestic violence, supervisors and managers, and the like. Such tips were notably missing from many of the training activities.

Training of frontline law enforcement personnel was the first phase of what constitutes community policing. Now it is important to concentrate on the other part of the equation of community policing: community residents and agencies. Community residents and other leaders, especially some who belonged to Neighborhood Watch groups, attended and benefited from many of the workshops. In subsequent years of the training and technical assistance, the net should be cast wider and include more strategies that incorporate community residents and agencies. Among the goals to attain in this regard is:

1. the broadening and thickening of networks linking law enforcement with various sectors of the community;

2. the dissemination of LASD-RCPI community policing information in pamphlets and newsletters distributed in neighborhood settings;

3. the initiation of research documenting community and police collaboration and implementation of effective strategies;

4. the formulation of workshops tailored to community needs and assessments, but still addressing topics such as gangs, domestic violence, introduction to community policing, and so on; and

5. the workshops should be organized and presented in the community settings such as service agencies, schools, or churches.

With the overarching purposes derived from the COPS mission in mind, initiatives that more closely link the community and police would go a long way toward ensuring that community policing becomes institutionalized in ways that problem solving cuts both ways. The police and community would be a part of the solution, or as one officer interviewed in the telephone survey put it: "Becoming more a part of the community as opposed to apart from it." It would gradually help to modify attitudes such as those of another officer, showing disdain for such strategies, who referred to community-oriented policing as "Hugs, not cuffs." The skills, attitudes, and knowledge base so important to community policing would cross the lines between public servants and private residents.

As always, change in any culture, including police culture, requires a total involvement, reexamination, and revamping of all participants in that culture and society. The LASD-RCPI training and technical assistance program has initiated culture change in new and innovative ways among law enforcement personnel. With the inclusion of community residents, another dimension of culture, community culture, would be changed to fulfill the goals of community policing.

chapter

4

Time

The time and effort most of us put into our life generally leads to results, which can be positive or negative depending on what we have exposure and access to and with whom we identify. For a conventional life, we learn a set of skills, acquire knowledge, and develop attitudes that become lifelong tools for survival and success. Parents strive to teach their children these things or introduce them to role models, guides, and resources that aid in the attainment of these goals. In neighborhoods where street socialization has taken over, these possibilities are considerably curtailed or lacking. In fact, it has been shown that the skills, knowledge, and attitudes that are shaped by the streets lead to a destructive, unconventional life.

Stealing *time* away from the urban youths most susceptible to street socialization and gang life is a difficult task. Such efforts involve programs and activities that target or involve the three most important social control institutions of our society: (1) homes and families, (2) schools and teachers, and (4) law enforcement and police. Time management is of the utmost importance. Time and timing are issues with respect to not only the general time available to youths, that is, with whom and where they spend it and what they do with it, but also the key points in their life that are pivotal to their growth and human development. Early and later childhood developments are sometimes filled with social and personal episodes that can plague a person for life. However, the adolescent years are the "heightened" time when developmental crossroads intersect to offer good and bad choices, turns and twists, dead ends, free-wheeling paths, and any number of alternatives that are momentous in their impact.

Start with the Home

In the realm of home/parents, school/teachers, and law enforce-ment/police, the home is the first in our time construct. It is the child's parents, or perhaps some other caregiver in the family, with whom the child establishes his or her first human contact. Gang research has shown that strained family life often involves little or no parenting, espe-cially where research (Vigil 2007) shows that parents are either over-worked or are hamstrung because many of their own childhood experiences have never been addressed or resolved. Therefore, homes and families often are not stable places in which children spend their early years. Rectifying this can and should start at the community level where various groups and agencies would meet to develop a collabora-tive, coordinated strategy for local families and parents.

Parental counseling initiatives would pull together existing programs and practitioners working in low-income areas to develop a curriculum to aid parents most in need. Candidate homes for *preventive* measures would be selected by identifying parenting voids reflecting strains, ine-qualities, and unsteady practices, and without stigmatizing them, to assist parents in connecting or reconnecting with their children in ways to have some influence over them. In effect, the counseling would center on the parents as individuals as well as on their roles as parents, with the child as the end recipient in order to break the cycle of pathology for those families that have children in gangs.

Parenting classes would augment counseling. Parental education is among the most vital of these goals (Dinkmeyer & McKay 1976; Patter-son 1975). Having never experienced this in their own youth, many par-ents lack an understanding of what constitutes good, sound parenting. For some parents, this type of training would go hand in hand with the counseling noted above; in fact, information and insights generated by the counseling sessions could easily serve as the basis for the parenting training. Because so many parents were very young themselves when they gave birth, they may benefit from learning about the authoritative approach successfully used in many nongang-affiliated families. This child-rearing strategy emphasizes attentive parents, firm rules, disciplin-ary follow-through, and a closed-ended schedule (e.g., a curfew). The parenting program could be designed and run by mothers within the neighborhood or by an outside entity such as a nonprofit agency. Proven strategies, such as setting appropriate limits and adequately supervising children, could be taught. In addition, other children in the household might be involved in the program for additional reinforcement as well as preparation for the future when they may be parents or caregivers.

Broader concerns should also be considered—such as the damage that multigenerational gang involvement has on family and individual prospects (Klein & Maxson 2006). Why are there emotional ties that bond individuals to a particular gang, for instance? In the event that youths will not be dissuaded from participating in gang activity, parents should remain as emotionally involved as possible in their children's lives, a practice that can be learned in parenting classes. Even if only a modest influence, parents can begin to show their children ways of gaining respect other than through gang association.

In addition to parenting classes, various other social, behavioral, and mental health services need to be provided to the parents of impoverished neighborhoods. Marriage counseling and general psychological services must be fashioned to address the cultural practices of the population (Alexander & Parsons 1982). More importantly, these services must be delivered in a manner that is culturally rooted to the entire neighborhood. As part of an extensive violence *prevention* program modeled on the adaptive principles of public health, we must unequivocally underscore the strong correlation between abuse and conflict in the home and the tendency toward violent gang activity on the streets. Many of the female family heads are stuck in cyclical relationships in which violence or abuse commonly occurs. Although a very complicated, difficult, and sensitive issue for many abused women to discuss, such behavior must stop, not only for the well-being of the women but also to eliminate the negative pathological example it sets for the children (Kruttschnitt et al. 1986).

Similarly, drug treatment centers must offer unrestricted treatment on demand for all residents, adults and youths alike, without regard to whether they are affiliated with gangs or not (Stanton, Todd & Associates 1982). Many families in low-income neighborhoods are plagued by drug or alcohol abuse problems of one sort or another. Indeed, drug use is rampant in such neighborhoods and only leads to greater apathy and increased violence. If multiple flexible modalities of drug rehabilitation treatment coupled with adequate social services and support programs were offered, it is likely that some of the gang activity would be curtailed or diverted. Nonetheless, this recommendation is made with the recognition that such a battle is not won easily or without serious change on other levels related to law enforcement practices, the economy, and parenting practices. For these and other reasons, the long-term success of drug-treatment programs is uncertain.

A final recommendation involves introducing residents to the world of possibilities that exist outside their living situations and conditions. Programs and mechanisms should be developed for residents to become more mobile and leave the area in order to experience new places, people, and activities. Access to affordable transportation would open up the residents' world beyond the borders of the barrio or ghetto. A connection

Waiting for the party
to start

with a larger society would improve psychological health, which inevitably affects all other elements of a life. After conducting research in a housing project, the author was able to help formulate such a program for youths ages 9 to 14 (Vigil 2007). IMPACTO (Imaginando Mañana: Pico-Aliso Community Teen Outreach) secured housing authority monies and a small grant from the Robert F. Kennedy Memorial to mentor and counsel both youths and families and to introduce the children to social and educational outings that took them to another world. The program has had moderate success and is still in operation as of this writing.

Generally speaking, a focus on homes and families is the first step in stealing time away from street socialization. Early on it is the home and family situation that dominates the life of budding gang members—who can be 8 or 9 years old—and sets them on their way to a destructive life. This focus on the home and family should be considered the starting point of a process that would continue with other social control influences.

Continue with Schools

Schools are the next most important arena that takes up the time of youths. Schooling affects the development of a person to adhere to the lifeways of our society. As we know so well, schools located in low-income gang neighborhoods have failed in this regard (Valencia 2002). Schooling for children in these neighborhoods has often been a process of disengagement and dropping out. More time is spent out of school, as the outside street world takes over. Below, I outline some of the practices and methods that would help set youths on the right path educationally (Vigil 1999; Vigil, Nguyen & Cheng 2004).

The repercussions from stressed families carry over onto learning and schooling. Schools are next in importance to the family in social control (i.e., societal equilibrium). They also usually represent society's first opportunity to participate in the socialization and development of its children. Where the family might fail or falter, somehow the public school must fill the void in fulfilling its obligatory role in socializing all youths. Parents must be encouraged and influenced to join teachers and participate in the dialogue and interaction necessary to guide and direct their children.

Children from unstable families residing in low-income, gang-oriented neighborhoods typically score poorly on tests and exhibit behavioral problems in the classroom, often compounded by street pressures that infiltrate the classroom (or at least the schoolyard). Conventional efforts at *intervention* through, for example, parent–teacher conferences, often meet with parental apathy, among other hindrances (Wang, Reynolds, & Walberg 1995). As these children get older and their behavioral problems become more serious, often influenced in that direction by gang membership, the usual institutional response is to attempt to suppress the problem behavior and/or to remove the child from the school (Moore 1978, 1991). This response not only often constitutes abandoning all hope in the child's future but also does little to prevent other children from following the same dysfunctional development.

Get Smart after Head Start in elementary school

Nevertheless, as Slavin, Karweit, and Madden (1989, p. 355) have pointed out: "Prevention and early intervention are much more promising than waiting for learning deficits to accumulate and only then providing remedial or special education services." Heeding this advice, a bold strategic plan must begin in the early grades, perhaps even in Head Start (preschool) (McKey et al. 1985), for example, with follow-up (or Follow Through, which is what it was referred to in War on Poverty programs of the 1960s) in elementary or middle school (Slavin et al. 1989; Vigil 1993).

Another issue is that the resultant innovative schooling strategies generally address the needs of "at-risk" children (Rossi 1994; Slavin et al. 1989; Wang et al. 1995; Waxman 1992). However, the various school-based strategies that have been formulated, and are constantly being reformulated, often miss the street-socialized segment of children. This stems, in part, from their focus on a "generic" at-risk child (Stein, Leinhardt, & Bickel 1989).

For now, suffice to say that sound *prevention* and *intervention* strategies follow basic educational thinking and human growth and development principles. Social, emotional, cognitive, and physical aspects of a child's development should be especially targeted. Respect, emphasis on positive reinforcement, attention to self-image, a democratic learning process, sensitivity to cultural differences and nuances, and recognition of the variation in student talent are just some of the factors to consider.

School time is crucial. There have been many innovative but unsuccessful efforts to keep adolescents in school. Any new ideas must have "teeth" in them but should not be unbalanced. For example, tracking low-achieving students by placing them in learning groups is a common practice among educators. However, this technique should be avoided because it reinforces the "grouping" tendency and pattern generally common to gang formation. Instead, individualized instruction should be attempted beginning with a personalized reading program that would use high-school-student and community-college volunteers who live in the neighborhood.

In fact, reading alone should be the primary focus in the early elementary years. If children do not learn the skills necessary for reading at this time, they will become disengaged in the process of learning in the later grades. For example, a time-intensive technique utilized by many kindergarten and first-grade teachers to aid students in reading development and to capture their interest in reading is to have each student compose a story about an incident or person in his or her life. The teacher writes the story as the student is telling it, and both of them discuss what illustrations should accompany the account. Here, the local volunteers play a role in the drawings and illustrations to construct the child's book. The student thus obtains a personal book from which to learn letters and words and to share with the other students, who have created similar teacher-aided stories.

The technique of having students compose a story echoes the ecocultural approach of researchers (Weisner 1997) who encourage an interview format that relies on the interviewee to set the tone and direction of the exchange. For example, the interview begins with, "Walk me through your day," thus allowing the interviewee to bring up issues of his or her own choosing. Moreover, students also gain from this the freedom to introduce elements and realities from their own lives into the educational process. The story and/or drawings provide the teacher with insights into the emotional and social life of the child. In this way, teachers are equipped with information about each child on which to base their teaching strategies. Furthermore, with the right, sensitive approach, these insights could be brought up during the parental counseling and training sessions.

Alternative schools, initially formulated to address the learning and behavioral difficulties of high school students, have devolved largely into an "intervention ploy" and, worse, a holding tank for all the wayward children of the area. Unfortunately, the grouping and tracking phenomena in the early grades are further strengthened when a student reaches an alternative or continuation high school. Here, putting all the students with serious problems together reaches a critical mass and generates a state of additional cohesion. It has become, as some observers have blatantly stated, a type of "soft jail." Sadly this sometimes goes beyond the metaphor. Jackson High School was an East Los Angeles school for bad boys in the 1930s. When school officials recently converted it to an elementary school they discovered a jail cell in the cellar.

Instead of creating more "soft jails," what we need to consider is keeping students in high school in a different, more structured way. Recent innovations in this area include a boot camp arrangement in a facility that can house the students 24/7. Students "self-select" for this schooling arrangement by nature of their *attitude* and *behavior*. For example, a football coach in Pico Rivera used to recruit gang members for the football team by virtue of their behavior. If he saw them doing something wrong, like stealing a purse, he considered it an act of courage and therefore anointed them as a football player. Self-selection of this sort, a kind of ethical ju-jitsu, with parental participation and approval can work. It is one possible recruitment mechanism for the volunteer boot camp learning module, which enlists students who have bad habits like tardiness and absenteeism, class disruption, streetlike gang behavior, and other forms of antischooling attitudes and acts.

A comprehensive and positive strategy of reaching out to marginalized students would thus go in the opposite direction of present-day school actions in which it is more common for school authorities to push or kick out students if they evidence gang attire or behavior. The boot camp approach would involve a type of grouping, which is admittedly a problem, but structure it in a way that every moment is accounted for in guiding and directing youths. (Boot camps will be discussed in more detail in chapter 5.)

Another example of changing problem behavior is demonstrated by the story of a high school principal who reached out and co-opted key individuals, converted them, and gained their cooperation to redirect and co-opt the street culture as a whole. In this example, in a suburban neighborhood of mostly Mexican Americans, a group of teenagers at the high school belonged to the local gang. The male principal, who had himself grown up poor and on the streets, approached a couple of the group's leaders one day and engaged them in conversation about why they just hung around the gym restrooms. He followed this up over the next few weeks with more discussions that strategically brought the other gang members into the picture. After a while, the group façade of the gang members melted away—a posturing for the group that became self-evident to gang counselors. The principal then asked them what they thought the school lacked in programs they would be interested in. A boxing program was initiated based on their requests. Later, the idea of a student-governing group to complement regular student-body activities was born. A Boy's Council was formed, made of marginal gang students, and they began to meet weekly to discuss matters of campus interest.

These examples demonstrate that, when you are able to communicate and interact with a gang member separate from the group, a different and often very vulnerable person emerges. Acknowledging this tendency, school officials and teachers should attempt to carefully separate and individualize the counseling and remediation of a pre-gang or gang member. The more private this contact can be, the more likely the individual behind the group-induced façade can be reached. With this opening, rapport is established and trust is gained; the child gains confidence to speak freely about his (or her) trials and tribulations. Materials from education courses on gangs give teachers constructive information that they can use to make sure children who have already bonded socially in the street do not have negative bonding further reinforced in the classroom.

There are many more ideas and examples where school officials and learning programs can make a difference in occupying the time of students. In sum, programs to keep students in school, off the streets, engage them in reading and learning, and help them to address the pervasive gang problem should be a priority.

The Role of Law Enforcement

If homes and families and schools and teachers have their role to play, then so does the law enforcement community and especially police

officers. Since the gangs have taken over where home and school influences have left off, by providing affection and nurture and instruction
and learning, police, and law enforcement in general, have stepped in as
"street social control specialists." For some out-of-control children, the
police are often the only controlling force in their lives and oddly sometimes the only role model they have.

This is particularly the case with police who have daily contact and
interaction with street populations. Learning from these interactions,
police departments in gang areas have developed several approaches and
programs that have worked. The most difficult goal for police is to get
gang members off the streets and involved in other outlets and, in so
doing, to nurture more mutually respectful police–youth relations. Plenty
of examples can be cited where the police served this role by making
social control a matter of providing prosocial places and activities for
children. In this way, the police presented a different face to the children
and community.

My childhood was positively affected by the DAPS (Deputy Auxiliary
Police of the Los Angeles Police Department) program, which was implemented in neighborhoods where gangs were rife. DAPS offered sports
and recreation as well as field trips. As other examples of youth-oriented
programs, the L.A. County Sheriff's Department started the Hollenbeck
Youth Center many years ago, and currently, the Youth Activity League
(Y.A.L.) exists in 10 of the 17 substations. The latter outreach program
offers sports, such as boxing, karate, flag football, and overnight camping
among many other educational and recreational activities.

Learning how to "rap"

Another example is the L.A. Sheriff's Community Oriented Policing Services (COPS) program. Having evaluated the COPS programs (see chapter 3), I can testify to their success and effectiveness. There are several components to COPS, but the primary goal is to narrow the gap between the police and community residents in ways to break the animosity that can exist between them. Bringing a type of "Officer Murphy" patrolling (patrolling a beat on foot and mingling with members of the neighborhood) back and implementing a community-based policing strategy has generated good will and opened lines of communication. Police come to be viewed by at-risk youth not as a threat or problem but as a part of the solution.

COPS is a "soft" *suppressive* strategy, and there have been many others that have been initiated but for one reason or another dropped. VIDA in the late 1990s was one—a Sheriff's program that was like a boot-camp experience for young first-time offenders. The late L.A. Bridges program (ended in 2008) brought parents, teachers, and police together to intervene with middle-school children. This was another fine idea that had been somewhat hamstrung—its weakness was that it was spread all over the city with only minimal funding, instead of just targeting gang infested neighborhoods.

The neighborhood drill team

Previous Anti-Gang Programs

Having observed all the anti-gang strategies over the last 30 years in Los Angeles, I can truthfully state that none of them have had lasting positive effects, either because of poor planning and implementation or inadequate funding. Starting in the early 1980s was the Community Youth Gang Services effort, borrowed from the Philadelphia Plan from that same city, which hired streetwise gang counselors as crisis intervention specialists in high-crime, gang neighborhoods. When the authorities and the public tired of this program, realizing that gang violence had actually gone up during its tenure, then another solution was sought. Enter in the late 1990s, the L.A. Bridges Program, which at least was multidimensional and focused on the crucial first years of middle school, but as noted above, it was eventually terminated. Today, a new even more comprehensive, coordinated initiative from the L.A. Mayor's office, known as the Gang Reduction & Youth Development program, is underway and shows promise as a broader strategy that might effectively address and alleviate a rather complex problem. There are 16 such programs in various parks throughout the city of Los Angeles. I visited one of them in August 2009. I came away very impressed with its "wrap around" array of activities and services, serving at least 200 residents from 6:00 PM to 11:00 PM, mostly children of all ages and a nice sprinkling of adults, but notably lacking were activities for gang members.

In effect, the above strategies have assisted the home, school, and law enforcement socialization routines in taking time away that would otherwise be spent in street socialization. Not just taking the time away but also replacing it with alternatives that build the habits and skills of a solid member of society. Sadly, up to now, street socialization has taken most of the time of youths, and this has forged hardened street gangs and hardened street gang members. If we can rob all or some of that time away, we can begin to shift this dynamic.

Following are some current programs that address the *time* element both in real time and in the timely life stage for prevention.

Suggested Programs

Varieties of Parental Education Programs

There are many existing programs of prevention, intervention, and suppression that have one thing in common: a focus on the child, with the aim to help him or her make correct decisions in life and steer clear of gangs. With the parental programs summarized here, the goal is to teach mostly the parents rather than the child. The whole thrust is that parents are the first and arguably biggest influence on a child's life. Because of this they should be accountable for striving to be proficient at raising a child. If successful, this child-rearing effort would limit the likelihood of the child growing up to be a gang member (Chanequa, 2001). In theory, this would eliminate the need for many other anti-gang programs simply by stopping the problem before it even gets started.

The general aim is to target marginalized populations throughout a city: first-generation Americans, parolees who are parents, and single parents who live in low-income areas. According to *Juvenile Delinquency: Theory, Practice, and Law*, by Siegel, Welsh, and Senna (2006, pp. 200–227), each group mentioned above, has anywhere from a slight to major chance of raising delinquent children who could become gang members.

First-generation Americans experience cultural strains, such as trying to raise children as though they are back in their respective country of origin, which put undue stress on a family. Although the practice of keeping one's own culture is a natural tendency, the idea of a family maintaining one's own culture in America often leads to familial strain and childhood confusion. American life requires new habits in family and gender roles and expectations. When first-generation parents enforce their cultural lifestyle on their children, it can marginalize them in school and put them at a higher risk for gang membership. Thus, immigrant parents need to balance their desire for intergenerational cultural continuity with an added dimension of careful acculturation.

On the one hand, it has been suggested (Siegel et al. 2006, p. 210) that family deviance is one of the most powerful indicators of juvenile delinquency, and that is why it is important to have programs that target *parolees*. Although other factors can be faulted, such as genetics, it is clear that lack of parent–child bonding due to parental incarceration, domestic violence, and the possibility of a child modeling him- or herself after a parent who is a criminal are parental circumstances that taint their child's development. On the other hand, it is common knowledge that a child benefits from having two parents. Children from families headed by a *single parent* are more likely to commit crime than children reared by a father and a mother (Siegel et al. 2006). This is because in single-parent households parents have a harder time supervising and spending time with their children, which is a key component for keeping children out of gangs (Vigil 2007). In general, families who live in low-income neighborhoods also are at risk of having delinquent children or children who are members of a gang, because these neighborhoods have a tendency to be violent (Chanequa 2001).

Programs that focus on informing and teaching parents about how to raise their children properly are in existence today. These include the prevention programs—*The Incredible Years, Strengthening Families, Families First,* and the *Proud Parenting Program*—and the intervention programs—*LIFT* and *Functional Family Therapy*. All of these programs have different takes on how families should be picked for their programs and how to deal with whatever problem is at hand. I will break down the highlights and goals of each of the above-mentioned programs to show the strengths and weaknesses.

The Incredible Years is a *prevention* program that targets aggressive and poorly behaved children ages 2–12 years. The strategy is to make them more socially competent at home and at school by employing five levels of courses. The courses take into account several factors, such as the family's socioeconomic status, the child's age, and if the family is from an ethnic minority population. This program involves family counseling, self-taught lessons with the aid of puppets, and homework for both the parents and the children. The idea of having different courses available depending on a family's characteristics and demographic makeup is a great idea, since there is no way that one program would work for every family. According to Spitzer (1991) The Incredible Years helps parents feel more in control of their children and teaches parents how to raise their children to be productive, well-behaved human beings.

Strengthening Families, a *prevention* program, focuses on building five protective factors into families. These five factors are (1) parental resilience, (2) social connections, (3) knowledge of parenting and child development, (4) concrete support in times of need, and (5) a child's specific social and emotional development. These five factors are essential ingredients for families to raise children and protect them from child abuse. According to Olson (2007), this program aids in establishing a stable family structure. Research shows that it is a very effective way to raise children, as children that go through the program are less likely to get into trouble with the law or experience child abuse. The only weakness is that there is little in the program that factors in cultural differences.

Families First is another *prevention* program that focuses directly on supporting and educating parents. This program understands that first-generation Americans have trouble adapting to American norms, in addition to communicating with their children. This program is great because it takes into account the parents' cultural backgrounds when teaching them to be better parents. Families First also includes teachers who are capable of speaking other languages. Parents that were enrolled in Families First (http://www.families-first.org) had increased their knowledge of and confidence in raising their own child, by practicing the lessons they learned at Families First. The program focuses on three areas of child development—discipline, self-esteem, and communication—which helps in successfully rearing children in this family-focused program.

The last example of a *prevention* program is the Proud Parenting Program, formerly known as the *The Young Men as Fathers Program* (http://www.cdcr.ca.gov/Divisions_Boards/CSA/CPP/Grants/PPP/Proud_Parenting_Program.html), offered to young parents ages 25 and under as well as to parolees who have children. This program focuses on three goals: (1) teaching parents that child maltreatment is closely linked to later delinquency and can be prevented, (2) young parents must be held accountable for their parenting obligations, and (3) being an involved parent is good for self-esteem and can be a motivating factor for a successful life. The program teaches parents through classroom instruction, participation in family activities, and teacher mentoring. This program focuses on the parents as the people who are the most influential in a child's life. Research demonstrates that when the program was still known as The Young Men as Fathers Program, many, if not all, of the young men that the program targeted severely lacked the knowledge, mind-set, and skills required to be successful fathers (Leavitt 1999).

LIFT, an *intervention* program, has an entirely different approach in helping families with troubled children. LIFT's philosophy is to help court-involved families (e.g., families in which a child has been arrested and tried for a crime) understand the juvenile justice court system by providing legal information and guidance so the family can navigate the system more easily, which is believed to increase the family's stability and to decrease the chances that they will ever have to return to court (http://www.liftonline.org/programevaluations.html).

Functional Family Therapy is another *intervention* program that takes at-risk youths ages 10–18 and their families and puts them into numerous counseling sessions. These sessions are often funded by state grants, so they are easily accessible to lower-income families and can even be used as an alternative for juvenile incarceration. The sessions outline goals that families can reach for and achieve by maintaining a positive parent–child relationship. As stated by Barnowski (2002), this program has been proven to work and is a great alternative to incarceration. When the program was fully completed by children who had been arrested and their parents, the offenders had a significantly lower recidivism rate than people who went through the justice system without additional help. Two shortcomings of the program are that it is mostly child-centered and focused on children who are *already* involved in the criminal justice system.

LA's BEST

LA's BEST (Better Educated Students for Tomorrow) focuses on the upbringing as well as the education of youths in Los Angeles County where "lack of parental supervision is one of the main causes of delinquency." The program mission of LA's BEST is to keep young children off the street after school. It was created in 1988 by the late, former Mayor Tom Bradley to address the lack of adult supervision of elementary school children ages 5 to 12 during the critical hours between 3:00 PM and 6:00 PM. Mayor Bradley grew up in an area of Los Angeles that was poor and full of street children; the Mateo gang was one of the most formidable in the neighborhood during his youth. The program provides safe and supervised after-school education, enrichment, and recreation, free of charge in elementary schools. It serves over 26,000 children, who have access to few resources, and many at-risk youths. Nearly 81 percent of the students who participate in this program are Hispanic, and 11 percent are African American. "Approximately 90% of the participants qualify for federal lunch subsidies" (Heckman & Sanger 2001).

In addition to lack of supervision, peer influence among these youngsters is significant. Since there are many gangs in these communities, children are bound to live in gang territory. Although the problem of why children living in low-income areas do not succeed in going on to the university is a concern of program leaders, the program's main purpose is to keep young children off the street after school. It has been a very effective program over the past years because there is a partnership between the City of Los Angeles and the Los Angeles Unified School District. Thus, community investment along with goals that align with prevention and intervention make this a successful program.

LA's BEST is a program that addresses two of the three most important social control institutions of our society: homes and families, and schools and teachers. This program provides young children with activities that enhance their ability to participate in school. It keeps them away from the dangerous streets of Los Angeles. It teaches them study habits and encourages them to find a hobby and make a commitment to their education. Staff members implement learning principles that allow the children to express what they already know and value their experiences and ideas. When the staff listen to and let students be involved in planning activities, they encourage students to participate and become engaged, making this program much more inclusive and successful.

When students are allowed to communicate their opinions, they learn communication skills and help establish achievable educational goals. Establishing this ideal early in life enables students to carry this knowledge into other aspects of life that require setting and accomplishing goals. They gain an inner confidence of knowing that they are respected and have their own identity, feelings they have not experienced in the past.

Below are some of the values (ought-to's) of the BEST program:

1. Nothing we do is as important as the effect it has on a child.

2. Engaging activities develop values, skills and relationships. Activities are not seen as ends in themselves, but as vehicles for creating values, building skills and solidifying peer and adult relationships. An engaging activity is one that holds children's attention, awakens their imagination, and inspires them to want to learn more.

3. All children have equal rights to be accepted, respected and valued by others. Children are viewed as individuals to be developed, not problems to be solved.

4. Children should be involved in decision making and program design. If children get to choose how, when, in what and with whom to be engaged, they are far more likely to enjoy themselves and behave cooperatively.

5. When we listen for understanding, everyone learns—children and adults alike. We are constantly able to learn from our children as well as each other. Everyone is a learner.

Head Start: The Earliest Prevention of Gang Membership

In 1965 the federal program "Head Start" began assisting families with services, which consist of much more than just a preschool and kindergarten-readiness curriculum (Palacios, 2008). In California alone, Head Start offers currently more than 121,000 poverty-stricken and at-risk children and their families a quality learning environment, health awareness, childhood development education, and nutritional guidance, as well as nutrition itself (see Early Childhood Knowledge and Learning Center: http://eclkc.ohs.acf.hss.gov/hslc). Vaccinations, health screenings, and dental care are also part of the family-oriented, comprehensive, and community-based program. Most importantly, it offers the enrolled families the most essential element of the Head Start Program, which is an approach to making a life difference: "social competence" (Palacios, 2008).

The program operates with the philosophy that a child will thrive with interdisciplinary programs that help the child develop normally and help detect and remedy any physical and psychological problems. Because readiness for primary education takes place in the home, it is a vital part of the program to integrate the parents and educate and aid them, not to simply replace them with child-care services. This approach provides tools to parents, who can then pass their understanding on to their children, becoming positive role models for them. A family united, socially and emotionally linked, creates an environment of trust and hope, in which everyone can reach achievements. The link between the program, other social service organizations in the community, the children, and their parents is intertwined with and reinforced by the program's continuous support of the entire family. When the children are well taken care off, the family experiences less stress and diminished health problems (Palacios, 2008).

Head Start is still greatly underfunded and can't reach all the children in need of its assistance. Two professors (Barnett & Hustedt 2004) who evaluated Head Start programs found supporting evidence that the overall program had lasting, long-term benefits. The researchers emphasized that a continuing increase in school achievement was observed in children who attended Head Start and furthermore stated that the impact of the program on the parents was very positive (Barnett & Hustedt 2004). The parents showed heightened belief in their children and increased positive behavior toward them, producing a better home environment for all family members. This is an indication of the social impact the program can have on modifying parents' belief system and behavior.

Results from a longitudinal study by Abbott-Shim and colleagues (2003) showed that parents of children who were enrolled in a Head Start program and therefore received health and preventive care demonstrated more positive health and safety habits for their children than did parents whose children did not attend Head Start. Head Start enrollment also showed statistically significant long-term effects for "vocabulary and phonemic awareness," giving the children an advantage in school and social functioning (Abbott-Shim et al. 2003). The addition of a preschool program to initiate the child's social journey into the school life brings a statistically significant result of social competence (Raut, 2003).

Generally, a prevention approach targets the problem at hand. However, the prevention of gang membership has no one solution but rather is multifaceted, due to how multiply marginalized the population at hand is (Vigil 2002). To meet a family's social structural needs, effective prevention requires a cumulative approach, including empowering the family and offering generational change, where previously unfavorable role modeling was the norm. Head Start's programs offer families guidance, eliminate unsupervised time in a child's life, educate the parents, and provide help with seeking other social services available in the community.

Head Start provides indigent families with the opportunity to send their children to a safe place while parents are working or getting an education, without the additional burden of day-care expenses or leaving children unattended and home alone (Palacios 2008). Children, who experience loneliness could feel abandoned and neglected. Feelings of abandonment often break the bond between children and their caregivers or role models. Intercepting this chain of events can prevent the need for peers to fill a void of social isolation otherwise created within the child due to lack of a positive adult influence and family cohesion. Head Start provides children with a safe and rich environment in which to interact with peers and get an education, preventing them from experiencing "street socialization" (Vigil 2002).

Head Start is a prevention program—prevention being "the approach to avoiding something from occurring" (Mish, 2004). Lavertue and Migneault (in Siegel et al. 2006) state that "crime prevention consists in proactive, non-punitive measures having the specific goal to reduce crime by removing the factors that promote it," thereby giving an initial course of action to stop gang membership and resulting delinquency before it starts. The "age-crime-curve," which depicts delinquency starting at or before age 10 and peaks at the age of 16, shows youths are at risk of committing delinquent acts starting at elementary school age or before (Siegel et al. 2006), and it is therefore imperative to intervene prior to the first antisocial acts. It is critical to socialize at-risk children at an age preceding entry into elementary school, using appropriate pre-school and prevention programs, such as Head Start.

Head Start aids in educating the parents in better socializing their children and providing support in the initial phase of their children's lives. With this primary aid by the program, families can avoid feeling frustrated, helpless, or beleaguered and build a stronger foundation to pass on to their children. This help might be the fist time parents them-selves have experienced the comfort of social support, having possibly been neglected and abused as children themselves, giving them a chance of breaking the cycle for the first time in their family's history.

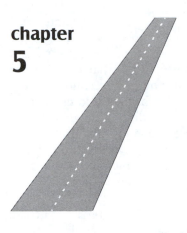

Place

Street socialization generally produces a street subculture of violence, and neighborhood "hot spots"—areas with a high concentration of crime—undergird a pattern of violence. The potential for street mayhem and violence in such places is a product of opportunity. A youth who spends more time with criminal offenders is more likely to participate in offending activities. In short, motivated offenders, suitable targets, and an absence of capable guardians converge in certain times and places to increase the possibility of a crime. Thus, social scientists have traditionally suggested that "hot spots" and a subculture of violence characterize violent and aggressive neighborhoods. In addition, however, the level of street socialization and *locura* (discussed in chapter 2) or "hot heads" in such places also raise the degree and intensity of heated affairs and the aura of violence.

Hot Spots and Contested Space

Place can be examined from at least two perspectives. First, there is the reality of certain "hot spots" as places where crime and violence peak. Second, there are the contested areas between gangs, which come in several forms. In one form, gang members proudly boast that they protect the actual space and their homes and women. In another form, there is symbolic space or "turf" that must be defended from pecuniary intruders set on controlling the drug market. Disputes over "market" space are rather recent and became more widespread when drug trafficking escalated in the 1980s and 1990s.

The police handled hot spots by stepping up patrol patterns and schedules to drive criminals out. But evidence shows that this just led the culprits to gravitate to another location where they continued the street group activity, criminal or otherwise. The hot spot, in essence, is mobile. There will always be hot spots, set or roving, in neighborhoods where there is a criminal element, like gangs. One example is the Pico Gardens housing project that was razed and rebuilt over a period of several years (1998–2003), with gang members selecting another hangout during the construction period. Gradually, the Cuatro Flats gang has returned to the turf, now with its new buildings.

The goal, then, is to lessen the impact of the elements that create the hot spots, and that is where the second purpose of the gang place can be addressed. The romantic notion of the gang as protector of the community, although still occasionally uttered by gang members, is a thing of the past. It may once have been true that gang members saw their purpose as defending their neighborhoods from other street people. Such strangers entered the premises to do harm to the homes and people there, especially the sisters and girlfriends who were considered fair game. However, with one gang conflict following on the heels of another over the decades, this explanation has lost its meaning. As gang fights and deaths accumulate, the new gang members merely learn that a certain neighborhood and gang is the enemy. Furthermore, as narcotics operations began to take over the streets, intruders became a matter of infringement into a gang's "business" territory.

Age-old gang conflicts and drug trafficking are the current raison d'être for the territorial/space tradition of the gang. Gang graffiti usually separates gang turfs but "tagger" graffiti lately has muddled the picture, so that gang members usually just have a general idea of the boundary markers between neighborhoods. Because of this blurred awareness, rival gangs often carry a roving notion of gang turf with them into any place where they might run into an enemy. As a result, some gang members might even claim a whole section of a city. Thus, the traditional idea of turf is no longer applicable.

However, drug trafficking as the dominant explanation for gang conflict shows a mixed record of evidence. In the 1980s it was discovered that the association between being a gang member and a drug seller was not a one-to-one correlation (Klein and Maxson 1994). Even though drug sales do occur in certain places and gang members are involved in the trafficking, it still is unclear if this is the primary reason for gang conflict over turf. In short, there likely are multiple explanations for the fact that today street gang life has become so riotous and unpredictable.

How to Recapture the Place

As mentioned above, one strategy for dispersing gang members is for police to increase their patrol efforts in a particular area or hot spot. Here is where a balanced strategy would complement the police as we step in to co-opt and transform gang neighborhoods and introduce (or reintroduce) other, more conventional socialization venues into this muddled mess. We would get rid of the present either/or approach to dealing with gang turf and set up situations (i.e., social and personal outlets) and conditions (i.e., buildings and safe houses) that reestablish the character and identity of the neighborhood.

Flag football in the barrio

In the 1950s there was a concerted effort to develop social clubs or car clubs in gang neighborhoods. For a while this initiative was making inroads. However, the effort could not be sustained and eventually died out. Gangs returned as before. According to some youth workers of that era, a new cohort did not replace the original cadre of dedicated club counselors. In effect, adult supervisors of the social clubs died out in the early 1960s. Today, the gang territories are too many to count and the boundary markers too blurred. There is such an explosion of gangs that the places where gangs are spawned and hang out need to be rethought if we are to adapt the old social club strategy. A new strategy would integrate some of the time dimensions noted in chapter 4, including parental, teacher, and police involvement. Refitted into these traditional social control institutions, new community clubs (e.g., offering sports, recreation, social outings, youth and parent counseling, job outreach, education/mentoring, community service, and so on) would be established in the places that need them the most.

During the 1960s' War on Poverty a similar idea was implemented in the form of the Teen Posts. The greater Los Angeles area had about 135 Teen Posts. In a presentation I made to South Central Los Angeles youth workers in the late 1980s, I asked if the Teen Posts were still around, and someone answered that there were five left in the city. The strength of this *place* was formidable because it drew gang members to it by offering minimum wage jobs; youths could work 25 hours a week in a neighborhood youth corps (NYC) program. This opportunity was in addition to the other services and programs mentioned above. Trained people who cared "stole time" in a supervised "place."

Although such a renewed "Teen Post" initiative seems like a tall order, something like this must be attempted. Its formulation, implementation, and evaluation must be community based with parents, teachers, and police working together to deliver a balanced program. A pilot program can serve as an initial trial to determine the effectiveness of the module, and funds and resources can be drawn from various entities, public and private, with a strong evaluation component to assess whether it is doing the job.

Girls' flag football at the park

We need not put all our eggs in one basket, however. As this larger initiative is developed and tested for effectiveness, there are other smaller prevention, intervention, and suppression actions that can make a difference. Indeed, if larger efforts cannot be mounted, we can and should reach for lower-hanging fruit. I once suggested that local libraries can become mobile and introduce bookmobiles (like the ubiquitous ice cream and produce trucks in low-income neighborhoods) that make weekly rounds to facilitate children checking out books, all with the parental support and participation; maybe inside the vehicle a volunteer could write and illustrate personal books for the children. These bookmobiles could also adapt technologies to help introduce and demonstrate the uses of computers and the Internet to bridge the Digital Divide that so often leaves less-fortunate people unfamiliar with and lacking access to services and information.

Structured Internet cafes could enable wireless access to information. Almost all gang neighborhoods have stable working poor households that could become safe houses or study centers that could help anchor the untethered children of the area. Existing youth clubs and programs, such as the Boys and Girls Club or the Boy Scouts, could be beefed up and augmented with additional resources and funds. When I was young, we had the Woodcraft Rangers (Vara-Ortiz 2007) in the elementary school and the Catholic Youth Organization (CYO) at the local mission church.

Boxing sponsored by the CYO

New Realities, Scenarios, and Scripts

The point of putting all these different realities in one general place is to saturate it by raining a multitude of positive influences—to bombard youths with many choices that can't help but bring rewards for them. We must make new realities, scenarios, and scripts if we want new dramas and acting performances from our children. Recapturing youths in this manner goes hand in hand with them saying YES to options that heretofore were nonexistent or minimal. Their time will be better spent in places that can make a difference.

Naysayers will raise various ideological arguments about these ideas being another bunch of "government programs." The best response is to point out that in addressing any problem we examine the facts and have the courage to think "out of the box" in the here and now and not impose ideological arguments that defy scientific evidence.

Places can be a cause of gangs. Poorer areas tend to have more gang activity, as resources are more limited in those areas. If we examine what happened in Los Angeles, we see that immigrants have long been marginalized. Once they began to migrate into white residential areas, the Anglo community also migrated away from them. In doing so they took with them their support and funding for schools in the area. The marginalized immigrant community was left yet again with overcrowded and underfunded schools. There is a long history of striving to escape from the poor areas with gangs, yet wherever the people go they continually become marginalized. Due to lack of funding, or decent living wages, it becomes nearly impossible for families to move out of the neighborhoods where gangs are prevalent. These areas are the ones where programs become the most necessary to show youths that there is another way of life other than crime.

What follows are descriptions of programs that touch on places that can facilitate interventions.

CASASTART

The program name is CASASTART (Center on Addiction and Substance Abuse Striving Together to Achieve Rewarding Tomorrows) and is based at Columbia University in New York City. Its primary focus is on outcomes for children ages 11–13 years who are in transition from childhood to adolescence and are subject to delinquency and criminal behavior, drugs, and illicit patterns. Counseling and social work strategies are emphasized in the interventions for these social problems in highly distressed neighborhoods. Caseworkers consider the intersection of community, family, school, peers, and individual habits. The program delivers integrated services to identified youths and all members of their households. Case managers collaborate closely with staff from criminal justice agencies, schools, and other community organizations to provide comprehensive services that target individual, peer group, family, and neighborhood risk factors. In addition, programs are locally planned and directed to fit the values and cultural background of the neighborhoods. To address multiple risk factors across domains, the following eight service components are identified as central to the CASASTART model, which offers:

1. case management to develop and implement individualized service plans for youths and others in the household and to act as mentors for the entire family, with caseloads kept small (13 to 18 families);

2. family services to enhance parenting skills, provide counseling, and encourage parental engagement in youth supervision and development;

3. education services to help youths succeed in school through tutoring and specialized programs as needed;

4. after-school and summer activities to provide positive peer group experiences and life skills;

5. mentoring to provide youths with positive adult role models and caring relationships with adults;

6. incentives to reward and encourage participation in youth development activities;

7. community-oriented policing and enhanced enforcement to create a safer neighborhood environment in which police are partners working with youths; and

8. criminal justice intervention to link youths who are in contact with the courts with positive neighborhood resources and development opportunities.

Research indicates that certain risk factors, especially when combined, greatly increase the likelihood that adolescents will engage in problem behaviors that jeopardize their healthy development (see www.casacolumbia.org/absolutenm/templates/AboutCASA.aspx?articleid=276). During early adolescence, these combined risk factors may have the greatest impact on the life chances of youths. The CASASTART intervention strategy seeks to target early adolescent youths who have the highest levels of risk for problem behaviors. By emphasizing comprehensive intervention strategies, CASASTART incorporates multiple theoretical orientations into the prevention of problem behaviors. Several components of the initiative focus on both social learning and strengthening prosocial bonds. For example, the mentoring component provides youths with positive adult role models. Youths are also directed into after-school and summer activities that provide positive prosocial peer group experiences. In addition, CASASTART seeks to strengthen social control in both the family and neighborhood domains by encouraging parents to actively engage in youth supervision and through community-oriented policing.

Three personal characteristics that are found in youths vulnerable to problem behavior are targeted: (1) low self-esteem, (2) alienation, and (2) risk taking. Attention is given to association with negative peers and positive peers to determine school risk and protective factors, particularly: problem behavior in school, school truancy, chronic absenteeism, educational strain, academic failure, grade-level promotion rates, school dropout rates, and grade point averages. Family risk and protective factors are examined as indicators of the parental monitoring and supervision construct. How well is the family organized, are they good caregivers, and do they provide support and a caring environment for attachment? Below is a summary of outcomes taken from follow-up studies of the CASASTART program

- CASASTART youths were significantly less likely than control group youths to be current users of any drugs, gateway drugs and stronger drugs and past users of any drugs and gateway drugs at the one-year follow-up.

- CASASTART youths were significantly less likely than the quasi-experimental youths to report lifetime use of any drugs and gateway drugs at the one-year follow-up.

- CASASTART youths were significantly less likely than control or quasi-experimental youths to report lifetime drug sales and less likely than control youths to report current drug sales at the one-year follow-up.

- CASASTART youths were significantly less likely than control youths to report violent crimes in the past year at the one-year follow-up.

- CASASTART youths reported significantly fewer delinquent peers, lower levels of peer instigation, lower levels of peer pressure, higher levels of positive peer support, and higher levels of participation in after-school learning activities, compared with youths in the control group at the one-year follow-up.

- Total school promotion levels for CASASTART youths were significantly higher compared with control group youths at the one-year follow-up.

- CASASTART did not significantly affect youths' report of parental supervision, family organization, or family support.

Boot Camp

Popular media portray military basic training, or boot camp, as a gruesome and "in-your-face" experience strictly conducted by unquestionable authoritative figures dressed in flawless military uniforms. Civilians, foreign to military subject matter and self-discipline, are bemused when they observe military personnel perform common tedious tasks, such as standing at attention, on guard, in front of a fallen soldier's tomb, in thunder and pouring rain. "How does that soldier do that?" they ask. Or, "What maintains a soldier's motivation to keep on going on a 10-mile march, carrying a heavy backpack after only three hours of sleep?" The abilities and the military discipline to perform tedious and strenuous tasks and follow orders unquestioningly are instilled and learned during basic training or "boot camp." Another name for this type of program, which is often associated with prisons, is "shock incarceration."

Boot camps adopt a philosophy that is strictly applied to different facets of development that include physical, emotional, social, and cognitive aspects of an individual. Armstrong (2004) explains that "[t]he underlying focus of boot camp programs lies within an earlier version of their name—shock incarceration" (p.10). The boot camp experience aims to shock an antisocial offender into another lifestyle that is more conventional. The design of shock incarceration is an effective application, involving all the necessary human senses and stressors, which "shocks" or allows opportunities for outside influences to affect vulnerable individuals undergoing its treatment.

Since the 1990s, there has been a significant increase in the establishment of boot-camp–inspired correctional programs. MacKenzie and Armstrong point out the "emergence of juvenile boot camps has indeed been a recent but explosive trend. Out of the thirty-eight boot camps we surveyed, we only found one boot camp, the Challenge Program in Texas, which started operating before the year 1990" (2004, p. 27). This may be due to the effective results boot camp programs produce as well as the public's perception of them as being "tough" on crime.

Several opinions of boot camp revolve around the notion that it ultimately teaches participants to kill enemy combatants. MacKenzie and Parent assert that notion, but they maintain that "the ultimate mission of military training—teaching killing skills and eliminating soldiers' reluctance to employ them—is not relevant" (2004, p. 18). The shock incarceration programs adopt the similar, if not the same, strict military atmosphere of basic military training, without the doctrines of warfare and killing skills. MacKenzie and Parent clarify what boot camp military atmosphere entails: "immediate obedience to command and unquestioning acceptance of authority" (2004, p. 18). *Cognitively*, a participant in a boot camp program would have to develop the obedience and discipline to follow commands, especially under stressful circumstances and conditions, and restrain emotions and maintain military bearing (i.e., maintain a military, emotionless, and professional appearance and attitude). *Socially*, the participant would need to interact professionally in various activities that include his or her peers in order to succeed, reinforcing the concept of teamwork. *Physically* the participant would become very fit, as many of boot camp activities require manual labor, physical corrective training (having to perform calisthenics when a rule is violated), and daily physical training (exercise).

Effacing the individuality of the person, the uniform structure of the military atmosphere, such as enforcing all participants to have the same haircut, to wear a uniform, and behave in a similar manner, diminishes the possibility of social discrimination merited by clothing, appearances, and behavior. The elimination of certain freedoms (e.g. choosing when to go to bed, what to wear, what to say, how to walk) forces the participants to abide by the same standards and rules.

Boot camps now also put more emphasis on cognitive, emotional, and social facets of development by focusing on the implementation of educational, vocational, rehabilitation, and aftercare training (Mackenzie & Armstrong, 2004). Felker and Bourque described the educational services available at some boot camp programs: "[The program] used an individualized educational course, which culminated in passage of the GED (General Educational Diploma). . . . [In another program, academic instruction] focused on teaching basic reading, writing, phonics, and math skills, . . . all the programs offered life skills or social adjustment curriculums" (1994, p. 154).

Several boot camps throughout the nation share similar goals, though there may be several differences in the programs, such as more time and resource allocation to education and vocational training than to manual labor and performing drills and participating in ceremonies. These differences in various boot camp programs produce different results for each respective boot camp. Armstrong points out that "critics of the boot camp model have theorized that because of the military atmosphere, drill, and hard physical labor . . . [participants] would leave these programs more hostile, aggressive, and antisocial than when they entered" (2004, p. 12). However, after an assessment of several boot camps and their participants, Armstrong found that "participants were more positive about their experience in the program than were control groups . . . [they] generally agreed that their experience in the program had taught them to be more self-disciplined and mature" (2004, p. 12).

In addition to education and vocational training, the military structure (e.g., the chain-of-command, containing units ranging from brigades, battalions, companies, platoons, squads, teams, etc.) provides leadership opportunities for its participants. A boot camp program located in California named Leadership, Esteem, Ability, and Discipline (LEAD) produced positive results by integrating military structure.

> Wards [participants] . . . considered LEAD's military milieu and leadership training to be important features. One of the program's most successful training techniques is the rotation of platoon leadership among all the wards. Wards were aware and supportive of this practice that allowed them leadership experiences and thus instilled in

them responsibility, self-confidence, and teamwork. (Bottcher &
Isorena 1996, p. 171)

The common goals of boot camps contribute to human development,
as leadership flows from the foundation of physical, emotional, cognitive,
and social skills. Self-leadership and leadership among others are necessary attributes when performing physical tasks (exercising despite feeling tired), when in emotionally taxing situations (maintaining military
bearing), when required to be cognitively in tune (choosing to obey
orders and manifesting military bearing), and using social skills (influ-
encing and interacting with others).

Here, an example of a boot camp is highlighted. *The Sunburst Youth
ChalleNGe Academy*, also popularly known as "Sunburst Academy," is
located in Los Alamitos Joint Forces Training Base, operated by the 40th
U.S. Infantry Division in Orange County, California. The letters "N" and
"G" are capitalized because the program is run by U.S. Army National
Guard drill instructors, and the cadets stay in the U.S. Army National
Guard's barracks, supervised by the drill instructors. Sunburst Academy is
among Orange County's fastest emerging boot camp programs, as it is
publicized in local television accounts and news articles. The boot camp
model is evident in its program's mission statement located on their official Web site: "The mission of the Sunburst ChalleNGe Program is to
intervene in and reclaim the lives of at-risk youth to produce program
graduates with the values, skills, education and self-discipline necessary to
succeed as adults and citizens in their community" (http:www.ngycp.org/
site/state/ca2/). Also located on the Web site is general information and
eligibility information. According to the program, it is a preventive rather
than a remedial at-risk youth program; it targets high-school dropouts
(16–18 years of age) who are unemployed, drug-free, and free of legal
entanglements (no felony adjudications/convictions, not awaiting trial,
or not currently in trial proceedings). The integrated core components of
the program are: "citizenship, academic excellence (GED/high school
diploma attainment), life-coping skills, service to community, health and
hygiene, job skills training, leadership/followership, and physical training." Sunburst Academy's program is a "22-week Residential Phase,
which includes the Pre-ChalleNGe Phase, . . . followed by a year-long
mentoring relationship with a specially trained member from each
youth's community."

Sunburst's Academy's mission statement and program description
state that its goals are to prevent and to intervene, only accepting youths
who are age 16 to 18 years old. Program eligibility considers the time
(age group of individuals), place (location of places that manifest street
gang culture), and people (individual/personal determinants) aspects of
the applicants. The Sunburst Academy has potential to curb gang influences on youths; however, this particular program's strict eligibility

requirements excludes youths who are engaged in drugs and unwilling to commit to the program.

Analyzing Sunburst Academy's program description and goals reveals the program focuses on being a place that intervenes with youths who are likely to fall into gang life and become street socialized. Shock incarceration (the boot camp model) and the circumstances of the new cadets that join Sunburst Academy prevent further digression toward street socialization and intervene with the cadets' growth and development. This process, in turn, suppresses deviant behavior because it instills a new work ethic, a new sense of responsibility, and a new behavior in general that cadets learn throughout their residential stay at the academy.

How does the multiple marginality framework apply to the boot camp model? Integrating the boot camp model with the four major aspects of ecology, social, culture, and psychology controls the possibility of an individual becoming street socialized. The ecological aspects of a military atmosphere in a boot camp controls for the strains of underclass culture, culture change, family stress, and differences due to the uniformity arrayed throughout all the individuals in the programs (e.g. uniforms, standard haircuts) and due to the fact the program reinforces positive values and nondiscrimination. Socially, the boot camp model provides for supervision and educational training on how to properly manage fear, how to be socially apt as a productive citizen, and how to eschew street influences. Cultural aspects are similar to the ecological aspects, as the street front (street identity's physical manifest—clothes, slang communication, symbols, etc.) is not allowed or present. Individuals must interact with each other using appropriate standards set by the program. This is accomplished through the constant supervision of the drill instructors. Psychological aspects are also controlled because of the positive educational, vocational, and leadership training cadets receive. This training contributes to the formation of a positive identity, deterring the formation of a street identity.

Social control explains how gangs become a major influence on an individual versus the influences of family, school, and the police. In sum, if families, schools, and police fail to influence an individual from becoming street socialized and falling into gang life, gangs will succeed in introducing young individuals to street life.

However, once the boot camp model is introduced to an individual during the prevention, intervention, or suppression stage, an individual's influences are controlled under positive circumstances that reinforce socially acceptable values, ultimately contributing to the positive facets of development. Recall from chapter 1, the figure depicting multiple marginality's effects on social control and compare it with the figure below, showing how the boot camp model leads an individual to positive influences that in turn lead to a productive life.

Instructors/Mentors

Leadership

Teamwork — Positive Social Interaction

Physical Training

Education

The boot camp model

One of the major themes integrated in boot camps is leadership. The concept of leadership, if appropriately exercised and taught, is able to thwart any negative influence, including gang and street life. In a televised news report, Jacquelin Toueg (2008) interviewed Cadet Washington at the Sunburst Academy: "And I feel like such an incredible change in my life, you know, and I've done a lot of bad things. So when I came here, it was the turnaround point for me." The boot camp model provides the opportunities to "turn around" youths, including those in danger of becoming street socialized.

G.R.E.A.T.

One program that has realized success in helping to solve the youth gang problem in various communities is the G.R.E.A.T (Gang Resistance Education and Training) program, which was started in 1991 by a collective effort of the U.S. Bureau of Alcohol, Tobacco, Firearms and Explosives (ATF) and the Phoenix Police Department. This program is a school-based, law-enforcement instructed learning environment for youths, with the prevention of gang involvement and delinquent behavior as its primary objective. It generally follows the model of D.A.R.E. (Drug Abuse Resistance Education) and Just Say No to drugs efforts. The primary objective of the G.R.E.A.T. program is to help adolescents avoid becoming members of gangs by teaching legitimate ways to achieve success and how to refrain from using violence to solve their problems.

G.R.E.A.T. is a curriculum taught by local law enforcement officers (LEOs) to youths starting at the middle-school level and is intended as immunization against delinquency. The LEOs of the G.R.E.A.T. program must go through a training program before they are officially certified to teach the curriculum to youths in the school. I think that having the LEOs go through courses of education specifically tailored to the program itself teaches the LEOs what experiences they can convey to the children. The National Training Committee (NTC) oversees and guides the operational procedures of all of the program's teams and committees.

Using LEOs to teach the G.R.E.A.T. curriculum ensures that experienced people reach the children. Furthermore, the LEOs often have had firsthand encounters with many of the students in the program, so they are already familiar with each other. The LEOs bring a significant presence into students' lives and can influence them onto the right track.

The G.R.E.A.T. nine-week curriculum administered to young students distracts them from the streets by not allowing them to constantly be free wheeling on the streets, giving them something much more positive in their lives to participate in. The program appears to be effective over a nine-week time period, because within this amount of time it can

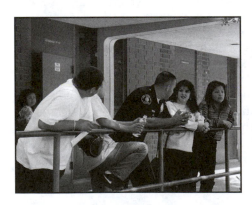

A cop counselor reaching out to youths

aid in changing the lifestyle of the student. Subsequently, the program repeats its core values over this time period to create a positive environment. The child can then compare his experience over time, with the old habits and values contrasted to the new ones. Over the nine weeks the parents as well as the students get to experience the benefits of the program. The communities, the families, and the students will have a new template for living, one that they can reflect back on to make corrections if old habits crop up again.

"The students completing G.R.E.A.T. reported lower levels of gang affiliation and delinquency than did comparison students" (Esbensen & Osgood 1999, p. 225). Through providing guidance and encouragement it offers alternative ways of thinking for youths who would otherwise be compelled to take the easy and familiar path of gang membership.

One of the four major goals in G.R.E.A.T.'s Strategic Plan is to "strengthen the relationship between law enforcement, school-aged children, and adults in the community." It allows for various opportunities for the officers to interact with the community outside of the classroom; it increases the number of families and law enforcement agencies that participate in the "Families Component," which is intended to strengthen the bond between urban youths and their families; and it develops partnerships with community organizations and business organizations that want to promote the G.R.E.A.T. program.

The G.R.E.A.T. Families Component uses group interaction, activities, and skills practices to engage parents and children ages 10 to 14 in order to foster positive family functioning. The G.R.E.A.T. connection with parents is especially useful. Not only are the youths of the program

The drill team does its thing

learning how to stay away from gangs but also the parents are becoming aware of what their children are doing over the course of training. By having the parents learn about the impact of gangs alongside the training, they will be inclined to be more protective of their children.

Woodcraft Rangers

Many groups have employed strong intervention strategies. One such group is the Woodcraft Rangers. Below is an outline of the foundations of Woodcraft Rangers.

In 1902, Ernest Thompson Seton, co-founder of the Boy Scouts (Adler, 2009), began the Woodcraft Rangers as an after-school program similar to the Boy Scouts. Seton got the idea for the program after a group of boys vandalized his farm in Connecticut. His goal was to deflect children from criminal activity by providing character-building opportunities based on the principles of service, truth, fortitude, and beauty. Cathie Mostovoy, chief executive officer of the Woodcraft Rangers, says "[the Woodcraft Rangers] honor that same mission today" (in Adler, 2009).

The Woodcraft Rangers was established in Los Angeles in 1915 and filed as a 501 nonprofit organization in 1922. Although the Woodcraft Rangers did not gain as much popularity as the heavily structured Boy Scouts, it remained an active youth group throughout the twentieth century. The program spread to different parts of the United States for different amounts of time, including New York, Boston, and Chicago, but now is primarily a Los Angeles–based group. In 1994, Woodcraft Rangers' Nvision After School Program (NASP) constructed after-school "clubs." Guillen-Woods (2003) explains that these clubs promote academic, physical, and social development. Further, NASP aims to extend schools' capacities to provide a safe and supportive environment after the school day and to help youths improve social, behavioral, and learning skills that contribute to academic achievement. The establishment of NASP marked the first strategy the Woodcraft Rangers used for students to achieve career goals.

The biggest dilemma here is that after-school programs must not make it seem like they are mere extensions of the school day. They need to be fun and challenging and make the students want to come back, instead of just keeping them in school for another few hours after the school day. NASP is designed to promote social and physical development with an emphasis on academic achievement (Guillen-Woods, 2003). Cathie Mostovoy suggests that the Woodcraft Rangers uses disguised learning, teaching literacy and math through activities like cooking and sports. Simon Lee says "kids are having fun—they don't know they're learning," and "[projects] come straight from the kids. We ask the kids what they want to do" (in Tepperman, 2008).

The Woodcraft Rangers has many goals achieved through a variety of activities. The Woodcraft Rangers Web site (http://www.woodcraftrangers.org) presents its list of goals. Its mission is to promote healthy youth development, especially in low-income neighborhoods that offer limited opportunities, "guiding young people as they explore pathways to purposeful lives." After-school programs and customized camping experiences enhance participants' social, cognitive, motor, and fitness skills. Woodcraft's programs also strengthen children's bonds with their natural support systems (schools, family, peers and community), thereby reducing their risks for academic failure, crime/gang involvement, substance abuse, and becoming teenage parents.

Moreover, the Woodcraft Rangers offers its programs during the afternoon, after school but before parents return from work, when students and young people are most vulnerable to dangerous peer pressures and risky behavior. The program encourages children from all ethnic backgrounds to join. As of this writing, the Woodcraft Rangers Web site states that the program consists of "81% Latinos, 12% African-Americans, 2% Caucasians, 1% each Asians/Pacific Islanders and American Indians, and 4% of mixed ethnicity. Participants are 51% female and 49% male." Programs implemented by NASP all follow the same structure:

1. Programs are offered in 8-week cycles that meet 3 to 5 days a week.

2. Programs run immediately after dismissal from school until 5:30 or 6:00 PM.

3. Programs begin with a 45-minute homework clinic where students can get hands-on homework help to complete assignments and establish positive study habits.

4. The homework clinic is followed by a 20-minute fitness activity and a nutritious snack.

5. Students then separate into their respective clubs and engage in a variety of club activities.

6. At the completion of each cycle, a recognition event is held to celebrate the students' accomplishments, which may include an exhibit, a team competition, a performance, or an awards ceremony.

The clubs are an integral part of the NASP programs. Students are encouraged to join two different clubs during each eight-week cycle so that they learn a variety of skills. Each time the club meets, students work on their respective skill set, with the goal of mastery at the end of the eight weeks.

Four clubs are currently implemented in NASP: (1) academic, (2) performing arts, (3) visual arts, and (4) sports. Club leaders can choose from a variety of fun themes within each club. For the academic club, the leader may choose from computers, science, poetry, cooking, children's literature, or children's math. For performing arts, themes include dance, cheerleading, drill team, drama, music, and puppetry. The visual arts leader may select photography, animation, model building, mural painting, drawing, or arts and crafts. The sports leader may choose basketball, football, volleyball, soccer, softball, martial arts, or fitness training. Leaders determine the theme based on the students' ages, genders, and age-appropriateness, as well as on students' interests and the staff's talents (Guillen-Woods, 2003).

Additionally, Woodcraft Rangers offers weekend day trips for children and parents. These include trips to educational, cultural, or recreational venues like museums, theaters, and sporting events. This offers parents an opportunity to connect with their children meaningfully by exploring activities in the Los Angeles area. For many children, "a Woodcraft Rangers field trip is their first journey outside of their neighborhoods." Also, a Youth Leadership Council offers students an opportunity to discuss strengths and weaknesses of the program, while developing leadership skills, improving the responsiveness of the program to student needs, and increasing club member participation. These meetings are useful to staff members, as they help plan new clubs and special events. Council members also enjoy occasional weekend retreats at Woodcraft's Stanley Ranch Camp.

Woodcraft Rangers currently offers a summer camp program in Blue Sky Meadow in the San Bernardino National Forest. This camp teaches children life and survival skills through a variety of outdoor activities including hiking, archery, stargazing, and nature studies. Children visit for a week at a time, with an expected 300 children for the three operating weeks during the 2009 season. Currently, fees are $370 per child per session, or $45 per child per session for qualifying children based on household family income.

Woodcraft Rangers has successfully reached several of its goals. While in the program, children are kept occupied during the most vulnerable time of the day: after school, before the parents get home. By intervening during this time, children receive positive, academic-based, achievement-oriented socialization, rather than street socialization. Many children and teenagers succumb to the pitfalls of street socialization by coincidence rather than necessity. When children are left unattended with nothing to do, they will explore options. Woodcraft Rangers directly addresses this problem. They keep students at school and give them something to do as an alternative to living on the streets.

It has been stated that developing a student's after-school activities into achievement-oriented life-skills training increases the child's resiliency. Keeping children in after school programs that focus on positive personal development is linked with promoting the skills and attitudes that help children handle the challenges in their lives.

It has been noted that children develop four main skill sets during these after-school programs:

1. social competence—forming positive relationships through communication, caring, compassion, and empathy;

Woodcraft Rangers skateboard seminar

2. autonomy—developing a sense of self through independent action, initiative, mastery, and a sense of personal power;

3. sense of purpose—feeling that the future will be positive through creativity, goal direction, motivation, and aspirations; and

4. problem solving—figuring things out that require critical thinking skills, flexibility, planning, and resourcefulness.

There also is a link to the increase in number of after-school activities with higher average GPAs of students.

These successes are compounded when parents get involved. Studies have shown that parental involvement in children's lives helps the children develop academically and socially. Children involved in the program are aware of their successes. Davontay Thomas of 99th Street Elementary School states how his life has changed because of the Woodcraft Rangers:

> If Woodcraft Rangers wasn't here at 99th Street, I don't think after-school time would be any fun. I don't think basketball would be fun like it is with Mr. Lyon, and we probably would have lost all our games. I like the fact that our coach treats us all the same and gives us the respect of a gentleman. Most of the kids at Woodcraft would be in a gang, and gangsters aren't getting anywhere, they're either dead or in jail, so if we didn't have Woodcraft Rangers, there would be lots of kids dead or in jail and they wouldn't know how it feels to be on a basketball team. (http://orangecounty.jobing.com/company_profile.asp?i=5026&viewMode=C)

Davontay realizes how the Woodcraft Rangers kept him out of a gang.

Present in Los Angeles for nearly a century, the Woodcraft Rangers has touched the lives of thousands of children. It maintains its passionate goal of being an effective intervention strategy to keep kids out of gangs. No single program can be a complete answer for gang intervention: more resources must be pooled to further combat this complicated problem. Although a balanced strategy of prevention, intervention, and suppression is necessary to eliminate the development of gangs in the inner-city, Woodcraft Rangers remains a forerunner in protecting children from the dangers and pitfalls of street socialization.

As we must note, the above programs definitely emphasize bringing changes to a place. In one instance, Boot Camp, youths actually go to a new place. Woodcraft Rangers and G.R.E.A.T. utilize the school and transform its purpose when their programs are taking place there. CASASTART attempts to be a program that operates as the intersection of neighborhood stakeholders—such as families, schools, community, peers—and individual habits. Social control institutions are key to place-based programs, as the families, schools, and police are considered very important.

chapter 6

People

It is self-evident by now that when time management is rearranged and the power of place reconfigured, people are the essence of the equation. Throughout the discussion of stealing time from and changing the place where youths congregate there were always parents, teachers, and police who are in the picture. In the last chapter, it was fairly obvious that caring and well-trained people can make a difference, provided that time was stolen from street socialization and new and expanded programs in certain places generated new socialization routines.

In gang neighborhoods there are numerous instances where adults and children exhibit actions and behavior that block efforts to guide someone to a conventional path. Indeed, there are too many examples where parents are absent and/or fail to care for and guide their children in appropriate ways. The case is similar for overburdened teachers in already overwhelmed schools or for police in highly stressed neighborhoods filled with too many destructive, negative activities. Despite these circumstances, many individuals in these same neighborhoods can serve as a supporting cast. Can we identify and recruit fathers and mothers to help other families if we develop the means to utilize their participation in a surrogate caring program? Are there young athletes in the locale who are trained and motivated to work with younger children in sports programs? Is there the will to identify, recruit, and utilize such leaders to help redirect children away from the gang world and the violence and destruction that destroys so many lives? If the prevention and intervention initiatives and resources were made available, there is no doubt in my mind that they would make a difference and accomplish a major change to curb or stop the gang mayhem.

After-school mentor training class

Folks in the Community

Particularly noteworthy in this regard is how community members could function to break the street socialization cycle that presently exists—where older street people embrace wayward children and, by their example, operate as street teachers and role models. With the aid of community leaders and residents this socialization network and matchup can be effected and measures taken to offer alternative, positive sources for emulation and direction. However, avoidance of stigmatizing these older street people as "bad" people is key to this overture. We can take advantage of the fact that most of the former gang members who have "matured out" of the gang (i.e., straightened their lives out) can be turned into role models; they now realize that they wish someone had made alternatives available for them.

Nevertheless, we need to be wary of the fact that many of these older gang-member role models have undergone deep gang socialization and could maintain a very strong antisocial and deviant mind-set. Thus, it is imperative that their presence and availability to unattached children be negated by the presentation of many other alternatives. In too many instances, it is these young and even older adults who strike the "loco" image that newcomers strive to live up to. For some children who become street socialized later in their teen years, it can be an especially significant pressure-filled situation that forces them to consume alcohol and/or ingest drugs to measure up to the loco standards around them.

Even when the gang dominates an area, nongang children still cite plenty of examples of school and church programs that have made a difference for them. For example, one 15-year-old male from East Los Angeles talked to me about how the police league took him to baseball games and the officer in charge always was asking about school sports and academic activities. This bimonthly contact and conversation was the only reminder he ever had of what benefits school had for him. When the teacher occasionally spoke directly to him, he would listen a little more carefully because of this reminder. In another case from South Central L.A., a 16-year-old male spoke of the local Catholic Church's after-school recreation programs. He stated that he always had something to do until dinnertime when his mother came home from work. All the siblings would gather at the table then to have supper together. A little homework and TV viewing would follow in his mother's presence. Such values as discipline, punctuality, hard work, family, respect, and loyalty were learned under these circumstances.

These routines and rhythms encourage and teach new skills, instill positive attitudes, and work to provide a viable and vital knowledge base for future troublesome situations. Self-respect, determination, courtesy, patience, responsibility, and other core values serve the individual to function more effectively in the social world around him or her. Other children, similar to those in the stories cited above, evinced this attitude and behavior and credited individuals and programs that gave them time and places for safe, constructive, and satisfying outlets. Oftentimes, children commented that some of the negative customs and habits they had learned at home or on the streets were countered and replaced by the positive, healthy ones that the program leaders had demonstrated. Thus,

A coach lines up
her team

children who were positively affected would spread the word to other children who were looking for safe outlets where fun and guidance could be found. Nevertheless, it must be noted that sometimes children who became gang members participated in these programs to no avail, as the pull of gang life was too strong for them to overcome.

As discussed in previous chapters, participation in programs can make a difference; the time "stolen" from a child and the safe places that provide prosocial activities in many ways gang-proof a child. Previously mentioned, were the Teen Post and NYC (Neighborhood Youth Corp) from the 1960s' War on Poverty. Having worked in the Teen Post program back then, I can attest that social/recreation programs in tandem with a minimum-wage job under the regular supervision and guidance of trained adults made a difference. Those who belonged to Jardin (a gang name taken from the tract name, Montebello Gardens—*jardin* is Spanish for garden) had less time for gang participation and activities. I returned to this barrio in 1986 to conduct research for the Bureau of the Census on the undercount of urban Latinos and reunited with several gang members, male and female, all of them now raising their own family (one female still possessed her black Teen Post sweatshirt). Our conversation reviewed the good times we had but also how the place (an old barrio building converted into several smaller offices and a number of recreation tables and spaces) kept us all busy, with at least four or five older teenagers and adults around, interacting daily with the more than 50 gang-affiliated youths. The Teen Post alumni were very appreciative of those times and people. Several other programs reviewed in this book have received similar positive comments, as we shall see with G.R.E.A.T., especially since this program presents police officers in a positive light.

In short, the pool of people available to join the fight for community health is potentially large. Heading the list are the residents of the community itself, parents, teachers, and police included. Members of poor but stable households, as noted above, can be tapped as community leaders. It is important to note, that up to 70 percent of all gang members eventually "mature out" of serious gang activity, and these individuals are a part of the community and can either help accelerate the process for youngsters at risk or be converted into becoming part of a positive solution. In other words, there are ways to recruit current and former gang members who have tired of the unpredictable, destructive street mayhem or have served time in detention institutions and undergone an awakening, to subvert the gang values and norms and assist the younger members in maturing out of the gang.

Former Gang Members as Street Counselors

In times past, there have been programs that recruited and screened former street gang members to help steer the new street generation away from gangs. The Community Youth Gang Services in the 1980s and early 1990s was one such Los Angeles effort. The 1960s' War on Poverty had a similar component in the aforementioned Teen Posts and youth outreach programs. The L.A. Bridges program, which lasted from 1997 to 2007, had integrated some aspects of this community philosophy in its operation, and there are many skeletal remnants of this practice in other areas of the city. In fact, the present program, Gang Reduction & Youth Development that replaced Bridges in 2007 has this component. The idea is a good one, but well considered improvements, reinforcement, and especially continuity are needed to fulfill its potential.

Because of certain scandals and irregularities associated with former gang members turned street counselors, many officials and citizens

A veterano puts his best
foot forward

frown on the idea of an ex-felon involved in a youth gang prevention or intervention program. However, if the screening process is carefully crafted, with parents, teachers, and police involved in the process, along with other members of the community, then many caring and informed individuals can be identified to help speed up the maturing-out process in gang-infested neighborhoods.

Especially important in formulating this facet of a balanced strategy is to ensure proper preparation and training for the selected persons who would provide the counsel and guidance to street youths. The concept is simple: if some of these guys are the OGs and veteranos whom the younger brood emulate and follow, why can't we co-opt the willing ones to direct youths in the other direction? It goes without saying that this is more likely to be successful if all the other recommended programs are in place, thus arming the reformed gang counselors with a menu of options and choices to steer the younger generation on a positive path. For example, while offering youths opportunities in sports training and other social enrichment venues, the streetwise counselor can look for trouble spots or detect when things are not right and step in to help rectify the situation. If necessary, this point man or woman could also recommend more in-depth counseling or other assistance when needed.

Programs

The programs that follow are examples that make a big difference because people help prevent the further advancement and institutionalization of street socialization and intervene to serve as role models and instructors who guide children in prosocial ways.

Baseball and Soccer

After-school sports programs have always had a positive effect on communities. They help build character in our children, as well as social skills, teamwork, and, of course, healthy bodies. Two examples of successful after-school sports programs are AYSO (American Youth Soccer Organization) and Little League Baseball/Softball. AYSO is a soccer league open to all for a small affordable fee, and financial assistance is also available when needed. It is designed as an after-school program targeted toward all ages but starts at age five and continues into high school. Little League Baseball/Softball also follows the same basic guidelines as AYSO; indeed, it pioneered the guidelines. Both programs provide a safe environment for kids to spend their after-school hours and provide a calm, relaxed environment in which they can take refuge from the busy and sometimes dangerous streets. These programs give children something to do on weekdays after school and help bring families together on weekends when games between teams are played. Importantly, the team coaches in these programs often serve as much needed adult role models for children who lack them.

The main point of AYSO and Little League Baseball/Softball is that everyone should be able to play and have an equal part on the team. They are designed so that the teams are fairly matched, so each team has a chance to win. These after-school programs are also designed to give children the chance to know each other and work on their teamwork skills, as well as deter delinquent behavior and promote productive behavior. These programs thus serve as a prevention tactic in developing a pathway that leads away from the street and delinquent behavior, including joining a gang.

While some youths will continue their participation in Little League and AYSO into their teens, such programs target mainly ages five to nine. They provide positive activity, in which both boys and girls can participate in a community setting, and promote parent involvement. Beth Miller, in *Critical Hours: After-School Programs and Educational Success* (2003), states that youths are particularly at risk during the weekday, from the hours of 3:00 PM to 6:00 PM, that is., from the time school lets out until parents return home from work. She analyzed both elementary and secondary school children. It is because of this big gap in time that Miller suggests that it is crucial to have organized after-school programs in order to keep children off the streets. Programs such as AYSO and Little League Baseball/Softball are the perfect thing for children to become engaged in. These sports provide an outlet for energy and an opportunity to learn and practice skills and positive behaviors from coaches who promote having fun within structured circumstances, including the limits and rules that pertain to the particular sport.

Midnight Basketball

Established in 1986 by the late G. Van Standifer, Midnight Basketball is a sports-based community crime-prevention program that encourages young African American at-risk males to play basketball from 10:00 PM to 2:00 AM as a prosocial alternative to drugs and crime (U.S. Department of Housing and Urban Development, 1994). It is imperative that no game begins before 10:00 PM in order to ensure that the youths are kept busy during the prime-time crime hours. This program operates only in the summer because it recognizes that crime rates are highest during these months. At least two uniformed police officers are present and visible at each game in order to control the situation if violence does erupt, especially due to the physically aggressive nature of the game (Hartmann & Depro 2006). These three basic components form the heart of the program, but there are additional factors that make it possible for this program to move toward progress in keeping youths off the streets.

By specifically targeting at-risk youth ranging from 17 to 21 years old, Midnight Basketball provides a safe, structured, and supportive alternative for young African-American at-risk males. It follows a soft suppression strategy that diverts those deeply involved in criminal activity from continuing their deviant behaviors. Soft suppression programs differ from hard suppression ones in that they are meant to guide targets away from gang life. On the other hand, hard suppression refers to gang injunction policies, such as having harsher sentences for being a gang member. In accordance with Hartmann and Depro (2006), cities that adopted the Midnight Basketball program experienced greater declines in crime rates than those cities that did not implement it.

The relative success of Midnight Basketball is not solely due to the fact that youths are given the chance to play basketball; there are other positive social forces at work within this program. For example, mandatory workshops by coaches and volunteers are given after practices and games in order to educate youths about important issues, such as substance abuse, sex education, and job interviews. It is also mandatory for all players to participate in every game, and the required man-to-man defense ensures a high degree of participation. Next, the media coverage, published box scores, official team jerseys, and supportive crowd turnouts further affirm the importance of the program in which families, schools, and law enforcement all play active roles.

Big Brothers/Big Sisters

To address poor self-esteem, the sense of free-falling in space, and limited hope for the future, youths can meet new people with whom they can spend some of their free time in new and different places. Filling such voids can help empower street children in different ways. This is where Big Brothers/Big Sisters of America (BBBS) comes in. It is largely a mentoring program, but an integral part involves a responsible adult volunteer taking his or her little brother or sister to fun and interesting places for exposure to a world outside of the neighborhood. This program has benefited many children and helped to take them off the streets.

Working as a clerk in a New York City courtroom in 1902, Ernest Coulter noticed that many young boys comprised a large number of the clients. Gangs were a serious problem then, and he thought these boys needed adult mentors to steer them in the right direction. He recruited 39 volunteers to work with different boys. By 1916, there were 96 cities with what by then was known as the Big Brothers; by 1977 it became known as the Big Brothers/Big Sisters of America.

BBBS is essentially a nonprofit organization whose sole purpose is mentoring young people. The organization targets youths between the ages of 6 and 18. These are ages at which youths can become susceptible to delinquent activities as reactions to inner-city life, neglect at home, and much more. Some of the children involved in the program are children who come from broken homes, experience poor living conditions, or who just need someone to talk to. Many of the BBBS centers are located throughout the country in both poor and middle-class areas, where they can reach out to young people.

BBBS relies on local people to volunteer. People who want to volunteer must first apply through the organization, and the application process is time consuming and thorough. Applicants are carefully screened. After applying, applicants are interviewed by someone from the organization and a background check is done. Additionally, the applicant must be able to provide at least two references. The agency needs to make sure the child's safety is not at risk and the volunteer is appropriate and willing to make the commitment. If the applicant meets all the necessary requirements, the agency will match him or her up with a child. The agency discusses the child's likes, dislikes, and other important aspects of the child with the volunteer in order to ensure a good match; the volunteer and child need to be compatible with each other. Some agencies also provide volunteer training so the volunteer can learn how to build an optimal relationship with a child and how to detect any trouble that the child might be experiencing, such as sexual abuse (Tierney, Grossman, & Resch 1995, p. 17).

The screening process is not only for volunteers but also for the children participating in the program. The child and his or her parent must submit an application and be interviewed together by the agency. A home assessment is conducted to better understand the child's needs.

Once the match is made, the agency continues to supervise the relationship between the child and the mentor. This is in order to see if there is any progress and also to make sure they are both meeting regularly with each other. The agency asks volunteers for only a small amount of their time—four hours per month for at least a year are required of volunteers. During these hours the child and volunteer meet and can do different activities, such as going to a baseball game or even just talking at the library.

Time is very important to the process. Regular meetings between the child and the mentor are necessary to build a good relationship between the two. The volunteer is not meant to be a tutor but rather a friend and someone to look up to. The child needs his or her mentor for guidance and being steered in the right direction. Meeting with each other regularly allows the child, who may come from an unstable background, to feel some stability in his or her life. Consistent meetings are also a constant reminder that there is someone out there who cares. It must be underscored that visits to other places, like the park, beach, movies, and mountains, are essential in setting a new social context for mentor–mentee interactions. These types of meetings are extremely important and the experiences shared there are key to building a long friendship. The meetings also keep the child occupied in a positive way—in a way that the child can escape from a life of instability and from being enticed down a wrong path.

The BBBS organization focuses on environmental factors, personal needs, and demographics. Environmental factors are external factors, such as family life. To determine which children are low risk and which are moderate to high risk, the agency looks at "children receiving free/reduced lunch, children with an incarcerated parent, and children not living with two parents" (Big Brothers Big/Sisters of America 2006, p. 15). Personal needs can involve aspects of life such as being poor or performing poorly in school. As for demographics, the agency hopes that the volunteers reflect the racial mix of each community's population.

A life of poverty and social instability characterizes these children. A major goal of BBBS is to reach 10 percent of all at-risk youth within each community it serves (Big Brothers Big Sisters of America 2006, p. 3). This translates to one million children nationwide. The organization plans to do this through two of its programs: the community-based mentoring program and the school-based mentoring program. The former involves parents and children reaching out to BBBS and the latter concerns BBBS recruiting schools and teachers. According to the "Making a Difference in School" report, which researched school-based mentoring, many of the children showed huge improvement. The children's academic performance improved, which included the "quality of the class work" and more assignments being turned in, and along with this, the number of absences also dropped. (Herrera 2007, p. iv).

Mentoring is clearly a wonderful and positive way to combat the gang problem America faces. Kids who are involved in gangs need someone to look up to and someone to give them hope so they can rise above their circumstances to reach their fullest potential. Mentoring is a great way to help kids stay away from gang involvement. BBBS provides mentorship that has an impact to help kids at risk stay off the streets by utilizing their time wisely and providing stability.

AVID

The AVID (Advancement Via Individual Determination) program has the goal of putting "students who are capable of completing rigorous curriculum but are falling short of their potential" into college-track classes. This program also aids the wider communities by helping kids stay in school and away from gangs—making them realize that higher education is an attainable goal. The possibility of attending college encourages these teens to stay focused in school and stay away from the pressure to join a gang or become involved in any activity that hinders their future success. I have had the pleasure of working with teenagers who are part of AVID at Estancia High School and Santa Fe High School. It is impressive to see the impact AVID has had on these kids and how hard these teachers are working. Achievement and success demonstrate that this program is one of the reasons why students are still in school and planning on going on to college. Even though both schools are in neighborhoods where gangs are rife, the support of the AVID program—teachers, tutors, parents, and other authorities—has made a difference. AVID is only the first step in increasing graduation rates and college enrolment.

Students at both high schools offered their opinion on the advantages of the program. The AVID program opens doors that would otherwise be shut to these students. The program gives them knowledge of the opportunities that are out there for them by introducing them to or encouraging them to enroll in college-track classes—such as advanced placement courses, honors classes, and elective courses that help them learn study skills and receive academic help. The students even attend tutorials where they get homework help. Through the AVID program, students receive help with college applications, practice SAT tests, and take trips to college campuses, places that most AVID students have never seen. This program changes the trend that exists in many low-income, rural, minority families of either dropping out or not continuing with their education because they either are not motivated or feel that they need to leave school to help their family.

The program is for children in grades 4 through 12 (between the ages of 10 and 17). It targets students who are in the fair to middle academic realm and may want to go to college. AVID has a middle-school program that instills a college-going mentality and prepares youngsters for the transition to high school. Getting these students interested in their future from the start motivates them to think outside of the box and set higher goals.

Over half of the students who are in the program in the U.S. are underrepresented minorities (Latinos and African Americans). AVID is offered nationwide in about 45 states and in about 15 countries, resulting in about 3,500 schools worldwide. The kids who are part of the AVID program take advantage of academic opportunities, and AVID ensures that they receive the same opportunities as the remainder of the student body.

Many AVID students realize that there is gang activity in their neighborhood and appreciate how inspirational teachers play a key role in keeping them away from such groups. Their teachers keep them up to date on when tutorials will take place, when there will be community service events, and any deadlines that are approaching. The students have to do a certain amount of community service per year in order to graduate. This helps them become more responsible adults and at the same time gets them more involved in their community.

One of the most important things AVID does is that is keeps students focused in school. Because of the fact that these students are taking more challenging courses they have to spend more time on homework and studying so they don't really have time to waste. By making sure that students do their work and attend tutorials AVID is minimizing the time these students have to be out in the street socializing and giving in to the peer pressure that is all around them. Part of the mission statement of the AVID program is to get students to "enter the mainstream activities of the school" (http://www.avidonline.org/).

Another way that AVID boosts students to heights they could only imagine is by bringing in motivational speakers to talk to students about the speakers' success stories. Sometimes a motivational speaker can get students to change their outlook on life because they hear firsthand about all the hardships that the person has overcome and realize that they want a better life. An example of this would be a speaker who comes in and talks about his previous involvement in gangs and how he matured out and found a responsible, prosocial path to follow. These are the kinds of stories that the students need to hear. Personal encounters are more powerful than having a teacher, parent, or other person tell them that gangs and drugs are bad.

The AVID program emphasizes giving the students all the support they need and has excellent host teachers who care about the students and their future. Students look up to their teachers and see them as mentors. The program also enlists college students as tutors. Most of these students are volunteers who offer to tutor the AVID students in all academic subjects and take time from their day to do so. When these kids see other minorities in higher positions, it is living proof that they can make it too. By giving these kids the role models they need, we are increasing the chances that they will stay in school and continue to become educated, responsible participants and leaders in a democratic society, which is also one of the aims of the program.

Parent participation is a big part of the program as well. Parents have to sign contracts that state that they will "support all AVID academic requirements" and attend meetings and events. Parent involvement in the program ensures that parents know their child's progress and that their child is at school, doing something productive instead of being out in the street.

Thanks to the AVID program, the rate of students going on to institutions of higher learning is increasing. When students are put into advanced placement classes they realize that someone believes that they have the potential, and this is a self-esteem booster that motivates students to try that much harder to reach higher levels than they did in the remedial and general education tracks.

One of the AVID teachers told me something that I found quite interesting. As we talked, he folded up a piece of paper and drew some lines on it, indicating three equal sections. In one section he wrote "dropout," in another, "high school diploma → work," and in the third, "college." He then folded the college section in half again and wrote "two year and four year" on it. As I watched him do this he told me about how the students in the dropout section are the ones for whom there are few programs, so they end up dropping out. In the second section are the students who plan on graduating from high school but do not continue after that. The AVID program helps some of the kids who either plan on dropping out or not continuing their education get to the third section and attend at least a two-year college. Unfortunately, it is not easy to get students to the four-year university section, but AVID is working on making these numbers grow and continues to make it possible for some of these kids.

As noted, parent participation is one of the essential features of AVID. Because of the threat of gangs in the area, parents are coming together to try to do something for the safety of their children. Parents want the Safety Resource Officer program to be implemented at their school, and to incorporate a somewhat community-oriented policing approach, which allows students and parents to get to know the officers and get comfortable with them. This program along with the AVID program at the school could help reduce the gang numbers a bit. By having a police officer on campus and by putting students at the academic level best suited to them, we are keeping them even further away from gangs and crime.

Homeboy Industries

Homeboy Industries is a nonprofit organization based in East Los Angeles whose primary objective is providing services that help give at-risk youths better opportunities to successfully reintegrate into a society that has rejected them (Fluidesign 2005). The goal of Homeboy Industries is to pull gang members away from deviant behavior and give them a chance to live a normal, fulfilling life. Homeboy Industries only employs at-risk individuals in its workforce (Iwata 2005). The company's executive director and founder, Father Gregory J. Boyle, started Homeboy Industries in 1992 in response to the civil unrest initiated by the Rodney King riots that were taking place in his church's neighborhood of Los Angeles (Fluidesign 2005). The program is located in Boyle Heights, an East L.A. neighborhood (Flores 2008) arguably with the highest concentration of gang activity in all of Los Angeles. For 16 years, Homeboy Industries has strenuously worked to significantly reduce the gang brutality that has taken place there.

Father Boyle believes if you can fix what the gang members are fleeing from, then you can correct the problem of gangs within Los Angeles (Barby 2008). Father Boyle underscores the motto of Homeboy Industries, "Nothing stops a bullet like a job," by providing job opportunities to those individuals who are involved in gangs or are affected by gang violence (Barby 2008). With the help of Father Boyle and Homeboy Industries, the streets of L.A. are slowly becoming a safer place to live.

Homeboy Industries staff

The organization benefits those who want to change their lives for the better but lack the necessary tools to do so. The Homeboy employees who have been drawn away from gang violence and illicit activities range in age from 14 all the way to 40. Homeboy Industries is a sanctuary for former gang members who yearn to become functioning members of society.

Homeboy Industries has developed interesting ways to help bolster social controls that prevent youths from turning to a life on the streets; these three social controls are family, police, and school. Father Boyle draws from a few widely accepted criminological theories, such as sub-cultural reference group explanations that hint at street socialization and socioeconomic strain that shows how poverty harms youth, which guide him in his decisions for how and where to prevent gang violence. Father Boyle applies these criminological theories in operating Homeboy Industries, and they influence how he draws at-risk individuals from gang life.

Homeboy Industries provides an effective counseling program that helps struggling youths overcome the problems that they encountered in a troublesome and sometimes abusive childhood (Fluidesign 2005). The counseling program helps its participants improve their family life, reintegrate successfully back to school, or develop the necessary skills to communicate successfully with the police. The counselors become a reliable alternative to the youths' so-called "brothers" on the streets. There are both female and male counselors because each gender deals with different sets of pressures on the streets of Los Angeles (Fluidesign 2005). Since leaving a gang is a struggle and an ongoing process, these counselors get to know the at-risk individuals on a personal level, and can even provide some personal experiences about gangs that support their advice (Fluidesign 2005).

To help address the school/education aspect of the social control institutions, Homeboy Industries provides its clients with a training program that can teach youths who have been socialized on the streets—affected by gang life—basic skills and transform them into productive members of the workforce. Many clients were deeply ensconced in a gang at a young age; as a result, they have little or no experience in vital skills such as reading, math, and interpersonal relations.

Probably the most important service that Homeboy Industries provides to its clients is the numerous job opportunities that give them a legitimate way of making money. Jobs take free time away from these at-risk youths, which they otherwise would be spending on the streets. Homeboy Industry's silk-screen and embroidery department is one of its older and most successful divisions since its inauguration (Fluidesign 2005). Started in 1996, the silk-screen department has employed 500 gang members and provided a working environment that places rival gang members together, forcing them to work side by side. Withholding anger in the workplace develops an attribute necessary for working and earning money legitimately in the future (Fluidesign 2005).

Homeboy Industries has recently announced its intentions of opening a bakery, which maintains the goal of training a select number of gang members in the lucrative trade of culinary art. The course begins by enrolling six former gang members in L.A. Trade Tech to learn the skill of cooking. Upon graduation from this trade school, the six former gang members will then learn from professionals during their required apprenticeship at well-known restaurants across the Los Angeles area. According to Father Boyle, "It is our purpose that this group will form the core of our future bakers" (Iwata 2005).

Homeboy Industries is well known throughout the Los Angeles area for its cheap and affordable landscaping and maintenance services. This area of employment helps at-risk individuals develop important traits, such as the ability to work with others in a team atmosphere, forming mutual respect, and learning responsibility for performing certain tasks. This sector of Homeboy Industries provides services to large accounts, such as the East L.A. Metro Project, the City of Los Angeles, and numerous residential and commercial properties.

The Homegirl Café, located in Boyle Heights, is open for breakfast and lunch from 7:00 AM to 5:00 PM. The staff primarily consists of former female gang members. The café helps give them an outlet from gang life that is not available to their male counterparts. The Bakery Department of Homeboy Industries will begin to service the Homegirl Café when the bakers have been sufficiently trained. The first phase of the Homegirl Café only seated 26 people, but the new 86-person café has received renowned praise throughout Los Angeles as one of the best restaurants in the area. The café has received shining reviews from *Oprah* magazine and the *Los Angeles Times* for its different twist on the normal food of the Latino heritage.

The most popular and well-known program, established in 1997, that Homeboy Industries provides is the Ya 'Stuvo Tattoo Removal Service. Removing tattoos is the first step in a long process toward successfully reintegrating into a society that expects its members to look a certain way. The service provides no-cost tattoo removals for those who wish to avoid being classified as a "no good gang banger" when attempting to enter the labor force. The Ya 'Stuvo Tattoo Removal Service draws clients, most of Mexican descent, from all over the Los Angeles area and has provided over 1,500 people with help in removing their tattoos. With the help of the Ya 'Stuvo Tattoo Removal Service, former gang members can erase their past and enter the workforce with no "visual" evidence of the lives that they have left behind.

Those former gang members who have gone through the Homeboy Industries program speak highly of it and Father Boyle. Gabriel Flores, a

Father Boyle and the homeboys

former gang member who now works in the Homeboy Industries silk-screen department, talks about how making money legitimately made him feel: "When I got my first paycheck, damn, it made me feel good. I didn't steal a car or sell drugs for money. I worked for it" (Iwata 2005). Flores is not the only former gang member who has positive things to say about Homeboy Industries. Grace Nieto, who was part of an all-girl gang in her youth, believes that "their job program is amazing. If it wasn't for them a lot of people, including myself, would never have had their lives changed" (Iwata 2005). These former deviants speak for hundreds of thousands of former and present gang members by expressing their appreciation for how Father Boyle and Homeboy Industries affected their lives.

Homeboy Industries will continue to grow and prosper for decades to come. Recently it has moved into a brand new 21,000 square-foot building in the heart of downtown Los Angeles. Homeboy Industries is now able to pull in an annual budget of $5 million through a combination of donations from private and public foundations. Some of the notable donors include Hollywood film producer Ray Stark and A&M Records cofounder Herb Alpert. When speaking about his new facility, Father Boyle exclaims, "It's going to transform the level of service we can offer. I'm excited to see where we can go from here" (Barby 2008). Father Boyle intends to keep expanding Homeboy Industries to reach out to the vast number of at-risk individuals within Los Angeles. Perhaps with a little more time and money Homeboy Industries can significantly reduce that number by a noticeable margin.

chapter 7

A Balanced Approach Would Work

Law enforcement and suppression tactics, already overtaxed as a solution to a problem they did not start, are having only moderate and uneven success in addressing the gang problem. It doesn't make any difference how many jails we build or how many cells are set aside for each new gang cohort, the strategy we now have has failed. It has failed because it is not based on facts, on science, on human development, or on common sense. We need to be honest in recognizing this fact and bold and courageous in charting a new course. A focus on the roots not the buds of the problem will generate logical solutions and aim not merely to stem the worst violence but also to begin the long hard march to regain social control. While the stick of punishment will have its role, emphasis will shift to introducing carrots and rewards early in a person's life—to balance the present formula to include prevention and intervention.

The long history of racism and poverty has had lingering effects on a number of levels, such as where people live and what types of jobs are available to them, which in turn affects the extent to which their family life is structured and organized to effectively participate in society. Many people affected by racism and poverty live in deteriorating neighborhoods, crowded conditions, and their children attend schools that have crumbling infrastructures, insufficient staff, and no resources to fix these problems. These, and other deprivations, result in the marginalization of these populations.

As suggested by the multiple marginality framework, linkages between place and status are clearly defined; for example, a smaller living

99

space makes for a crowded household and thus an increased propensity to seek room and privacy in public arenas like the streets. Gang life histories and other personal accounts make clear that time spent with other street people is in places such as rooftops, alleyways, parked cars, secluded schoolyards, and street corners. The limited space at home is often enough of a motivation to distance oneself from home, and when the household strains and instabilities are added to the equation, the personal need for getting out is increased. This often leads youths to seek refuge in gangs.

Woodcraft Rangers make low riders from bike leftovers

Moreover, racism and poverty tend to create stressful relations with law enforcement insofar as poor people often receive short shrift from authorities; there remains a sentiment of distrust and fear of the police among African Americans and Latinos. A great majority of the gang youngsters have had brushes with the law, and their overall attitude toward police is hostile. Among gang members, the consensus is that police are always hassling them (Vigil 1988a), and hardly anything positive transpires between them. Coming from lawbreakers, these reactions, of course, make perfectly good sense. However, the reaction, attitude, and sentiment of many law-abiding poor, ethnic minority residents are generally the same (Davis 1990). This makes for poor police–community relations, full of recriminations and spiteful charges rather than open and constructive feedback and communication. Imagined and fabricated incidents on both sides often overtake and dominate the dialogue; this further hardens attitudes. Are there ways to change this?

The soft suppression ideas mentioned in this text have practical advantages in turning around the troubling history that has cast a dark cloud over the community. Police can develop programs and services that involve the community. They can participate in youth programs to reach preteen children before they become gang members and it's too late. The G.R.E.A.T. program (police educating and modeling for youth) discussed in chapter 5 is a successful example of this police–community endeavor. Any program that presents the police in a favorable light is a win-win situation where contemporary victories are garnered while additionally helping wipe out the memories of the past by embarking on a new future.

When we brainstorm new ways to solve the gang problem, let us break out of the "hard suppression" box, and implement "soft suppression programs" such as G.R.E.A.T., boot camps, and sports programs (Little League, soccer, Midnight Basketball, etc.) that occupy *time*, provide a safe *place*, and expose youths to *people* who want to help—volunteers, educators, community members, and people who are hired to protect and serve. What better secure, stable entity could there be than law enforcement personnel to augment the prevention and intervention programs?

A Reconsideration of the Role of Place and Status

The integrative multiple marginality framework described in chapter 1 provides depth and width to a broad canvas to show why and how there are social control breakdowns and the many factors that need to be considered when searching for solutions. Ecological, socioeconomic, sociocultural, and sociopsychological marginality factors additively affect some members of particularly low-income, ethnic minority groups. These factors all intersect with one another and force some struggling families to adopt maladaptive, destructive behavior. To understand any of the forces at work here, it is necessary to understand all of them and to target them in a broadly based strategy.

Any initiatives undertaken should be understood as a societal strategy for the good of all, and coordination and cooperation is of the utmost importance in assuring its success (Klein & Maxson 2006). Thus, a macro approach is suggested for the partnership of public and private entities in formulating, implementing, and evaluating gang programs. Specific micro objectives can aim at the ecological, economic, social, cultural, and psychological details, particularly as they affect families, schools, and law enforcement.

One America Needs a Balanced Strategy

In the modern era there is no silver bullet to rid ourselves of our gang problem. Long ago at the inception of this "boy" problem in L.A., Bogardus (1926) made suggestions about family strains of immigrants, recreational needs, and improved police–community relations. Amazingly, these recommendations ring true today. The marginalization process of immigrant children then, so similar to what occurs today, necessitated a whole series of remedies. In the absence of these remedies, the marginalization process will continue to produce street gangs; avoidance of "social surgery" has evolved into a serious social problem. Because these relatively modest measures to address a budding problem were never taken, a more serious effort must be mounted today.

Needed today to address gang problems (and other social problems as well) is a balance of prevention, intervention, and law enforcement (Coolbaugh & Hansel 2000; Goldstein and Huff 1993), the carrots and

Kids with a police mentor

sticks that enable parents to help their children conform. We must begin to think of the children of our society, particularly the less fortunate, as ours to care for at an early age. Detractors will claim that this strategy is unworkable, impractical, and if implemented, another "expensive" form of welfare. Failing to realize that the present criminal justice apparatus is also a form of welfare, criminal justice welfare, these naysayers forget that hundreds of billions of dollars are spent every year to warehouse hundreds of thousands of largely poor, ethnic minority people (Blumstein, Cohen, & Miller 1980; Mauer 1992; Petersilia 1992). Sadly, this continues to be the approach in spite of studies that show the cost and benefits of early intervention and prevention tactics far surpass in savings those of the current strategy (Greenwood et al. 1996; Rubin 1999).

Few parents think that sticks alone can help them raise their child; neither should we expect that just getting tougher on crime, à la "three strikes" policies, can make a major difference (Elkannman 1996). Nor should we start off with sticks and then throw in carrots later, as most experts state that extremes and inconsistencies create great problems in child-rearing outcomes (Fraser 1997; Stouthamer-Loeber & Loeber 1986). Can we afford to not adopt a more balanced approach with all the children of the "one" America that is our society?

Start with the littlest and youngest

Law enforcement, of course, will always have to be a part of the maintenance of social control. Such extraordinary force is necessary at times to stem nonconformist behavior of a harmful or destructive variety. But it should not be a permanently asymmetrical approach to street gangs. In the last 20 years, or longer, law enforcement has had virtually unparalleled public support to address the gang problem. Only recently, and sheepishly, have some law enforcement leaders begun to question policies that rely solely on suppression and recognize that it is the roots, not the buds, that need to be the focus of gang eradication efforts.

Traditionally, the nature of the public debate has forced experts and observers to stake out an either "tough" or "soft" position on this problem, when a balanced prevention, intervention, law enforcement strategy is what is needed. Why not take this broader, reflective approach and be "smart" on helping youths find alternatives to gangs and crime?

References

Abbott-Shim, M., Lambert, R., & McCarty, F. (2003). A comparison of school readiness outcomes for children randomly assigned to a Head Start program and the program's wait list. *Journal of Education for Students Placed at Risk, 8*(2), 191–214.

Adler, A. (2009). Woodcraft Rangers move indoors for school programs. *Wave Newspapers*. Retrieved July 18, 2009, from http://www.wavenewspapers.com/news/local/39826227.html

Alexander, J. F. & Parsons, B. V. (1982). *Functional family therapy*. Monterey, CA: Brooks/Cole.

Alonso, A. (1999). *Territoriality among African-American street gangs in Los Angeles* (Unpublished master's thesis). University of Southern California, Los Angeles.

Alonso, A. (2010). Community dynamics and geographical descriptors of gang injunctions safety zones. Paper presented at the Academy of Criminal Justice Sciences, February, San Diego, CA.

Armstrong, G. S. (2004). Boot camps as a correctional option. In D. L. MacKenzie & G. S. Armstrong (Eds.), *Correctional boot camps: Military basic training or model for corrections?* (pp. 7–15). Thousand Oaks, CA: Sage.

Barby, C. (2008, May 15). Father figure. *Good Magazine*. Retrieved from http://www.goodmagazine.com/section/Portraits/father_figure

Barnett, W. S., & Hustedt, J. T. (2004). Head Start's lasting benefits. *Infants & Young Children, 18*, 16–24.

Barnowski, R. (2002). Washington State's implementation of functional family therapy for juvenile offenders: preliminary findings. *Washington State Institute for Public Policy, 85*, 56–79.

Big Brothers Big Sisters of America. (2006). *2007–2010 nationwide strategic direction*. Retrieved May 20, 2008, from http://www.bbbs.org/atf/cf/%7B1D98620C-CB6F-4825-A0AC-6E5BDFFC78E5%7D/2007-2010%20BBBS%20Nationwide%20Strategic%20Direction2.pdf

Bloch H. A., & Neiderhoffer, A. (1958). *The gang: A study in adolescent behavior.* New York: Philosophical Library.

Blumstein, A., Cohen, J., & Miller, H. (1980). Demographically disaggregated projections of prison populations. *Journal of Criminal Justice, 8,* 1–25.

Bogardus, E. S. (1926). *The city boy and his problems.* Los Angeles: House of Ralston, Rotary Club of Los Angeles.

Bottcher, J. & Isorena, T. (1996). First-year evaluation of the California Youth Authority Boot Camp. In D. MacKenzie & E Herbert (Eds.), *Correctional boot camps: A tough intermediate sanction* (pp. 159–178). Washington, DC: National Institute of Justice.

Bursik, R. J., Jr., & Grasmick, H. G. (1995). Defining gangs and gang behavior. In M. W. Klein, C. Maxson, & J. Miller (Eds.), *The modern gang reader* (pp. 8–13). Los Angeles: Roxbury.

Cartwright, D. S., et al. (1975). *Gang delinquency.* Monterey, CA: Brooks/Cole.

Chanequa, J. (2001). Ethnic differences in the effect of parenting on gang involvement and gang delinquency: A longitudinal, hierarchical linear modeling perspective. *Child Development, 72,* 1814–1831.

Coolbaugh, K., & Hansel, C. J. (2000, March). The comprehensive strategy: Lessons learned from the pilot sites. *OJJDP Juvenile Justice Bulletin.* Washington, DC: U.S. Department of Justice, Office of Juvenile Justice and Delinquency Prevention.

Covey, H. C., Menard, S., & Franzese, R. J. (1992). *Juvenile gangs.* Springfield, IL: Charles C. Thomas.

Curry, G. D., Richard, A. B., & Fox, R. J. (1994). *Gang crimes and law enforcement recordkeeping.* Washington, DC: U.S. Department of Justice, National Institute of Justice, Research in Brief.

Davis, M. (1990). *City of quartz: Excavating the future of Los Angeles.* London: Pimlico.

Decker, S. H., & Van Winkle, B. (1996). *Life in the gang: Family, friends, and violence.* New York: Cambridge University Press.

Dinkmeyer, D., & McKay, G. (1976). *Systematic training for effective parenting: Parent's handbook.* Circle Pines, MN: American Guidance Service.

Edgerton, R. B. (1978). *Deviant behavior and cultural theory.* Reading, MA: Addison-Wesley.

Elkannman, P. T. (1996). *The tough on crime myth: Real solutions to cut crime.* New York: Plenum Press.

Erikson, E. (1968). Psychosocial identity. In D. Sills (Ed.), *International encyclopedia of the social sciences* (vol. 7, pp. 61–65). New York: Macmillan.

Esbensen, F., & Osgood, D. (1999). Gang resistance education and training (G.R.E.A.T.): Results from the national evaluation. *Journal of Research in Crime and Delinquency, 36,* 194–225.

Esbensen F., & Winfree L. T., Jr. (2001). Race and gender differences between gang and nongang youths. In J. Miller, C. L. Maxson, & M. W. Klein (Eds.), *The modern gang reader* (2nd ed., pp. 106–120). Los Angeles: Roxbury.

Felker, D. B., & Bourque, B. B. (1994). The development of boot camps in the juvenile justice system: Implementation of three demonstration programs. In D. L. MacKenzie & E. E. Hebert (Eds.), *Correctional boot camps: A tough intermediate sanction* (pp. 143–158). Washington, DC: National Institute of Justice.

Flores, E. J. (2008). Homeboy Industries. *Los Angeles Times.* Retrieved May 18, 2008, from http://www.nytimes.com/slideshow/2008/03/19/business/0319-EDGE_ready_7.html

Fluidesign. (2005). Homeboy Industries. Retrieved May 18, 2008, from http://www.homeboy-industries.org/index.php

Fraser, B. J. (1997). NARST's expansion, internationalization and cross-nationalization (1996 Annual Meeting Presidential Address). *NARST News, 40*(1), 3–4.

Goldstein, A., & Huff, C. R. (1993). *The gang intervention handbook*. Champaign, IL: Research Press.

Greenwood, P. W., Model, K. E., Rydell, C. P., & Chiesa, J. (1996). *Diverting children from a life of crime: Measuring costs and benefits*. Santa Monica, CA: Rand.

Guillen-Woods, B. F. (2003). *A profile of the evaluation of Woodcraft Rangers' Nvision After School Program*. Cambridge: Harvard Family Research Project, HGSE.

Hagedorn, J. (2008). *A world of gangs: Armed young men and gangsta culture*. Minneapolis: University of Minnesota Press.

Hartmann, D., & Depro, B. (2006). Rethinking sports-based community crime prevention: A preliminary analysis of the relationship between midnight basketball and urban crime rates. *Journal of Sport and Social Issues, 30*(2), 180–196.

Hazlehurst, K., & Hazlehurst, C. (1998). *Gangs and youth subcultures: International explorations*. New Brunswick, NJ: Transaction Pub.

Heckman, P., & Sanger, C. (2001, April). LA's BEST: Beyond school as usual. *Educational Leadership, 58*(7), 46–49.

Herrera, E. (2007). Public/private ventures. *Making a difference in schools: The Big Brothers Big Sisters school-based mentoring impact study*. Retrieved May 24, 2008, from http://www.ppv.org/ppv/publications/assets/220_publication.pdf

Hirschi, T., & Gottfredson, M. (1983). Age and the explanation of crime. *American Journal of Sociology, 89*(3), 552–584.

Hofferth, S. L., & Sandberg, J. F. (2001). How American children spend their time. *Journal of Marriage and the Family, 63*(2), 295–308.

Howell, J. C., & Hawkins, J. D. (1998). Prevention of youth violence. In M. Tonry & M. Moore (Eds.), *Youth violence: A review of research, crime and justice* (vol. 24, pp. 263–316). Chicago: University of Chicago Press.

Iwata, E. (2005) Homeboy Industries goes gang buster. *USA Today*. Retrieved May 17, 2008, from http://www.usatoday.com/money/smallbusiness/2005-07-10-homeboy-usat_x.htm

Klein, M. (1971). *Street gangs and street workers*. Englewood Cliffs, NJ: Prentice-Hall.

Klein, M. (1995). *The American street gang*. New York: Oxford University Press.

Klein, M. W., & Maxson, C. L. (1994). Gangs and cocaine trafficking. In D. L. MacKenzie & C. D. Uchida (Eds.), *Drugs and the criminal justice system: Evaluating public policy initiatives* (pp. 136–148). Newbury Park, CA: Sage.

Klein, M. W., & Maxson, C. L. (2006). *Street gang patterns and policies*. New York: Oxford University Press.

Kruttschnitt, C., Heath, L. & Ward, D. A. (1986). Family violence, television viewing habits and other adolescent experiences related to violent criminal behavior. *Criminology, 24*(2), 201–233.

Leavitt, J. (1999). Fostering a more supportive society. *California Voter, 82*, 4–10.

Lovell, R., & Pope, C. E. (1993). Recreational interventions. In A. P. Goldstein & C. R. Huff (Eds.), *The gang intervention handbook*. Champaign, IL: Research Press.

MacKenzie, D. L., & Armstrong, G. S. (Eds.). (2004). *Correctional boot camps: Military basic training or a model for corrections?* Thousand Oaks, CA: Sage.

MacKenzie, D. L., & Hebert, E. E. (1996). *Correctional boot camps: A tough intermediate sanction*. Washington, DC: National Institute of Justice.

MacKenzie, D. L., & Parent, D. G. (2004). Boot camp prisons for your offenders. In D. L. MacKenzie & G. S. Armstrong (Eds.), *Correctional boot camps: Military basic training or a model for corrections?* (pp. 16–25). Thousand Oaks, CA: Sage.

Mauer, M. (1992). *Americans behind bars: One year later.* Washington, DC: The Sentencing Project.

McKey, R., Condelli, L., Ganson, H., et al. (1985). *The impact of Head Start on children, families, and communities. Final report of the Head Start Evaluation, Synthesis, and Utilization Project.* Washington, DC: U.S. Department of Health and Human Services.

Miller, B. M. (2003, May). *Critical hours: Afterschool programs and educational success.* Brookline, MA: Author. Commissioned by the Nellie Mae Education Foundation and retrieved November 24, 2009, from http://www.nmefdn.org/uploads/Critical_Hours.pdf

Miller, W. B. (1958). Lower class culture as a generating milieu of gang delinquency. *Journal of Social Issues, 14*(3), 419–435.

Mish, F. C. (Ed.). (2004). *The Merriam-Webster dictionary.* Springfield, MA: Merriam-Webster.

Moore, J. W. (1978). *Homeboys.* Philadelphia: Temple University Press.

Moore, J. W. (1991). *Going down to the barrio: Homeboys and homegirls in change.* Philadelphia: Temple University Press.

Olson, M. (2007). Strengthening families: Community strategies that work. *Young Children, 62,* 26–32.

Palacios, L. (2008). *Giving children a Head Start.* Retrieved April 11, 2008, from http://www.ochsinc.org/

Patterson, G. R. (1975). *Families: Applications of social learning to family life* (rev. ed.). Champaign, IL: Research Press.

Petersilia, J. (1992). Crime and punishment in California: Full cells, empty pockets, and questionable benefits. In J. Steinberg, D. Lyon, & N. Vaiaina (Eds.), *Urban America: Policy choices for Los Angeles and the nation.* Santa Monica: Rand.

Raut, L. K. (2003). *Long-term effects of preschool investment on school performance and labor market outcome.* Fullerton: California State University.

Rossi, A. S. (Ed). (1994). *Sexuality across the life course.* Chicago: The John D. and Catherine T. MacArthur Foundation Series on Mental Health and Development, Studies on Successful Midlife Development.

Rubin, E. L. (1999). *Minimizing harm: A new crime policy for America.* Boulder, CO: Westview.

Rumberger, R. W. (2002). Chicano dropouts: A review of research and policy issues. In R. Valencia (Ed.), *Chicano school failure and success* (2nd ed.). London: The Falmer Press.

Shakur, S. (a.k.a. Monster Kody). (1993). *Monster: The autobiography of an L.A. gang member.* New York: Atlantic Monthly Press.

Short, J. (1996). Personal, gang, and community careers. In C. R. Huff (Ed.), *Gangs in America* (2nd ed., pp. 3–11). Thousand Oaks, CA: Sage

Short, J. (2001). Youth collectivities and violence. In S. White (Ed.), *Handbook of youth and justice* (pp. 237–264). New York: Kluwer Academic/Plenum.

Siegel, L. J., Welsh, B. C., & Senna, J. J. (2006). *Juvenile delinquency: Theory, practice, and law* (9th ed.). Belmont, CA: Thompson/Wadsworth.

Slavin, R. E., Karweit, N. L., & Madden, N. A. (Eds.). (1989). *Effective programs for children at risk.* Boston: Allyn & Bacon.

Spano, J. (2007, October 25). 18 members of MacArthur Park gang are indicted. *Los Angeles Times,* B3.

Spitzer, A. (1991). Coping with conduct-problem children: Parents gaining knowledge and control. *Journal of Clinical Child Psychology, 20,* 413–427.

Stanton, M. D., Todd, T. C., & Associates. (1982). *The family therapy of drug abuse and addiction.* New York: Guilford Press.

Stein, M. K., Leinhardt, G., & Bickel, W. (1989). Instructional issues for teaching students at risk. In R. E. Slavin, N. L. Keswelt, & N. A. Madden et al. (Eds), *Effective programs for students at risk* (pp. 145–194). Boston: Allyn & Bacon.

Stouthamer-Loeber, M., & Loeber, R. (1986). Boys who lie. *Journal of Abnormal Child Psychology, 14,* 551–564.

Szanton Blanc, C., et al. (1995). *Urban children in distress: Global predicaments and innovative strategies.* Florence, Italy: UNICEF.

Tepperman, J. (2008). Serving so many more kids. *Children's Advocate* (March–April), 1–11.

Thornberry, T. P. (2001). Risk factors for gang membership. In J. Miller, C. L. Maxson, & M. W. Klein (Eds.), *The modern gang reader* (2nd ed.). Los Angeles: Roxbury.

Tienda, M., & Wilson, W. J. (Eds.). (2002). *Youth in cities: A cross-national perspective.* New York: Cambridge University Press.

Tierney, J. P., Grossman, J. B., & Resch, N. L. (1995). *Making a difference: An impact study of Big Brothers Big Sisters.* Philadelphia: Private/Public Ventures.

Toueg, J. (2008). *National Guard Sunburst Youth Academy.* Retrieved May 9, 2009, from http://www.youtube.com/watch?v=j3dehuyxhlu&feature=related

U.S. Department of Housing and Urban Development. (1994). *Midnight basketball: How to give young people a chance.* Washington, DC: U.S. Government Printing Office.

Valencia, R. R. (2002). Chicano school failure and success: Research and policy agendas for the 2000s (2nd ed). London: The Falmer Press.

Vara-Ortiz, F. (2007, November 12). Building bikes keeps teen "out of the streets." *Los Angeles Times,* p. B3.

Vigil, J. D. (1987). Street socialization, locura behavior, and violence among Chicano gang members. In J. Kraus et al. (Eds.), *Violence and homicide in Hispanic communities* (pp. 231–241). Washington, DC: National Institute of Mental Health.

Vigil, J. D. (1988a). *Barrio gangs: Street life and identity in Southern California.* Austin: University of Texas Press

Vigil, J. D. (1988b). Group processes and street identity: Adolescent Chicano gang members. *Ethos, 16*(4), 421–445.

Vigil, J. D. (1993). Gangs, social control, and ethnicity: Ways to redirect street youth. In S. B. Heath & M. W. McLaughlin (Eds.), *Identify and inner-city youth: Beyond ethnicity and gender* (pp. 95–112). New York: Teachers College, Columbia University Press.

Vigil, J. D. (1996). Street baptism: Chicano gang initiation. *Human Organization, 55*(2), 149–153.

Vigil, J. D. (1997). *Personas Mexicanas: Chicano highschoolers in a changing Los Angeles.* Ft. Worth/Dallas: Harcourt Brace.

Vigil, J. D. (1999). Streets and schools: How educators can help Chicano marginalized gang youth. *Harvard Educational Review, 69*(3), 270–288.

Vigil, J. D. (2002). *A rainbow of gangs: Street cultures in the mega-city.* Austin: University of Texas Press.

Vigil, J. D. (2007). *The projects.* Austin: University of Texas Press.

Vigil, J., Nguyen, T., & Cheng, J. (2004). Asian Americans on the streets: Strategies for prevention and intervention. *NEXUS: Journal of Asian Americans and Pacific Islanders: Policy, Practice, and Community, 1*(1).

Wang, M. C., Reynolds, M., & Walberg, H. J. (1995). *Handbook of special and remedial education: Research and practice.* New York: Elsevier.

Waxman, H. C. (1992). Reversing the cycle of educational failure for students in at-risk school environments. In H. C. Waxman et al. (Eds.), *Students at risk in at-risk schools: Improving environments for learning.* Newbury Park, CA: Corwin.

Weisner, T. S. (1997). The ecocultural project of human development: Why ethnography and its findings matters. *Ethos, 25*(2), 177–190.

Whitten, N. E., Jr. (1996). Ethnogenesis. In D. Levinson & M. Ember (Eds.), *Encyclopedia of cultural anthropology* (vol. 2). New York: Henry Holt.

Index